A whimsy about the author.

What should have been:

Petra Ceason was born on Wednesday 21 June 1972, on the right side of the tracks in a small town just outside Bristol. She was the first member of her family for several generations to fail to get into an Academically Biased institution, which left a severe, but deeply hidden open wound, until she was emergency blind dated with an older man. Although the wound took years to heal completely, Easteruprising O'Grady packed it with salve and sewed the edges back tightly together, on their first date.

She embarked on a passionately friendly Sexual Education Affair with Pi, until Mr. Right came knocking barely two months later. They were married when he graduated and she joined him in the frozen North, where they now live, with their two children, on the Estate he manages.

Pi, now retired, and with no children of his own that he is aware of, is a God Parent of each of the youngsters and a regular, and eagerly awaited, welcome-visitor to the house.

What is:

Rita -- Who? is chronologically parallel to more than a dozen novels and novellas about other personnel of West Novochester.

Also by Petra Ceason

West Novochester Chronicles Group

Karen, The Girl Who Would Be A Plumber.
Delia, Chef In A Wheelchair.
Janie, Mechanic On A Motorbike.

Rough Cut, Nearly Finished

Rosalind and Timothy, An Essay In Deflated Self Worth.
Frank, An Essay On Health.
Richard, Jim And Friends, Finance And Fine Art.

Work Related to Creative Writing Course

Collected Short Stories and Pomes.
{And No. It's not a typo.}

Work In Progress

Anna, CEO In Short Socks.
Ash and Cindy.
Fred and Louise, Reluctant Athletes.
Jane.
Jennifer and Sylvie, Flouting Convention, But Politely.
Jill.
Jo.
Pealle, Sporty Sparks.
Shelley and William, Autistic Artist.
Shirley and John.
Stewart and Jean.

Autobiography {Whimsy}

Writes En Passion.

Petra Ceason

Rita -- Who?

Rita -- WHO?

First paperback edition printed 2014 in the United Kingdom
A catalogue record for this book is available from the British Library.

ISBN 978-0-9930419-4-5

Published by Double Sausage
For more copies of this book, please contact Lulu: www.lulu.com

Designed and Set by Petra Ceason: www.petraceason.co.uk

Printed in Great Britain by Anthony Rowe.

Acknowledgements:
My thanks to My Tutor Mr. E. E Hughes for setting a 1,500 word homework from which a 60,000 word novel, like Topsy, just growed.

Ownership.

Petra Ceason™ is Trademarked as from 24/07/2014 and any shortening mis-spelling or representation of Petra Ceason.

Double-Sausage™ is Trademarked as from 24/07/2014.

Mervyn Waine™ is Trademarked as from 24/07/2014 and any shortening mis-spelling or representation of Mervyn Waine.

Mervyn Waine asserts the moral right to be regarded as creator of this work.

Jennifer Jackson Rods Co. Ltd.™ is Trademarked as from 24/07/2014 and any shortening or representation of

Jennifer Jackson Rods Co, Ltd.

Original Set in Georgia 12 point and other fonts. This version in whatever I could get away with, in my eyes the constraints imposed by ePub make the Spanish Inquisition look like a ultra-liberal social service!

If the Ancestor had ever owned a boat, he would have called it, The Double Sausage.

The publication of this First Commercial Edition funded by Double-Sausage.

Petra Ceason 2014

Author's Comment

Careers Officers apart, the Events and characters in this story are fictitious, any similarity to things that really happened and real people is purely accidental.

My **acknowledgements** and thanks to an early Twentieth Century edition of Boy's Own Paper, for a vaguely remembered story idea, that I adapted to become that of Mary Richards, fighting for her life in America's Old West. My **apologies** to Native Americans who, at that time, were portrayed as anarchic savages and thus also in the extract. I do know that contrary to the Hollywood Studio image, you had every provocation to wage war on the invaders, compared to many of whom you were civilised; my apologies also to the Wham-O Toy Company for turning their trade-marked name into a verb on Page 57.

My thanks also to my tutor Mr E. E. Hughes for the imagination stimulus picture of the four men meeting, from which all this sprang. My first effort you castigated, so did my Canadian dolly, even I wasn't that keen!

I like this one a bit better!

Careers Officer 'Gerald' once nearly destroyed a young girl, one of Himself's very own! These days, I am delighted to say, they are more like Norma.

This version has not been professionally edited, so I apologize in advance for my misuse of the comma. Anyone who feels strongly enough to contact me about this no doubt will find a way to do so.

I write the stories but, my characters' wild-child behaviour, free thinking and non-mainstream exploits are very largely their own. To avoid losing out completely, I have to hang on tightly, while they jump up and down. {To misquote Lonnie Donegan.}

I'm not sure that I always come out on top; consequently views expressed by characters in this book are always theirs, but they are occasionally mine too.

Petra Ceason

July 2014

Acknowledgements

I write separate scenes and join them up later, with invisible mending of varying quality. When J. K. Rowling acknowledged that that was how she wrote ‘The Philosopher’s Stone,’ it gave me heart to learn that the other writer who wrote at least one of her books this way was a Billionaire.

IT’S A PUsillanimous little American billion

of course, but what the floppies!

I for one wouldn’t mind being ninety-nine pence in the £ behind her.

To all those authors over the years who have given me so much pleasure a sincere and heartfelt thank you.

Arthur Ransome; Dick Francis; Robert A. Heinlein; Reginald Hill;
Jane Austen; Lew Matthews; Manning O’Brine; Dornford Yeats;
John Wyndham; C. S. Forester; J. K. Rowling to name but a few.

I have tried to credit you when I knowingly referred to your work. When I missed, it was innocently done, please forgive.

With so many wonderful stories buried in my cortex, I must have used variations on your ideas sometime.

Where I did so without credits, it was unintentional, and anyway, imitation is the sincerest form of flattery, even when done by accident.

Many times between writing and getting a scene to the printer, I too have seen one of my plot lines appear on the small screen.

One of my heroines asks of her boss,

“Have you got my brain bugged?”[1]

There are times when I think mine is.

Anyway,

Thank You! And where necessary,

Sorry!

Petra Ceason 2014

---

[1] Karen Robinson: Karen The Girl That Would Be A Plumber. Petra Ceason

For:

Gareth Mervyn Waine who loves to argue.
Especially when his standpoint is obviously untenable
and with no merit whatever.
Of course, when Rita was first written
he was fifteen, what do you expect?

And Susan Burn.
You savaged the first draft and justifiably so!
I hope you like this version.

And Norma, who went out of her way
to help me and my chicks for years.

And, as always:
Don't blame me,
blame Petra.
She did it,
all I did was hit the keys,

Mervyn Waine.

Rita -- Who?

Chapter 1

August 1984

Rita

The house was empty, neither gone to the shops empty, nor out to lunch empty, but not known at this address empty.

It was a sunny Saturday evening in a neat Council Estate in Novochester when Rita Roundheels thankfully turned into her street. She was only a few minutes from dropping the heavy rucksack down at her Dad's feet.

Although grubby, smelling strongly of wood-smoke and tired, the deeply tanned Girl Guide was smiling happily. It had been a good camp, she had several amusing anecdotes to tell John while she unpacked and sorted her gear out for the wash. She was looking forward to the luxury of a long soak in a hot bath, while her tea was made for her and then being subjected to a torrid time in bed, before a nights sleep undisturbed by cawing crows, carousing choristers, or clanking cowbells.

Home came into view round the bend and the prospect of a pleasant, languorous evening and passionate night, melted away as she got nearer.

She knocked anyway, but merely for form's sake, she'd known for certain by the time she turned into the gate, long before no-one opened the door to her approach.

The soul-less stare of windows with no people behind them was a complete giveaway.

Rita cased the house. The only possibility was above the canopy over the front door. The fanlight in the little bedroom window was open. The bedroom that she hadn't slept in since her Mum left. She'd done it before, as John well knew, she could do it again easily. He was probably counting on her doing it again.

"Wednesday night," said the neighbour over the garden fence: "Well Thursday morning, two-o-clock, John said he'd told you."

"Did he leave me my key?"

"Said he'd handed them in." Rita smiled thinly at the gossip and checked again, around the house. Her way in was either head first through her bedroom window, or tail first. Or --

"Could I borrow a window key please, just for a couple of minutes?"

"Back door key? They're all the same all over the estate."

"That's why John changed it." The neighbour returned with the window key, which would also open every window on the estate, but they hadn't needed replacing because to use it, presumably, you were already on the inside.

Rita shinned up the telegraph pole and, lemur-like, leapt from it across the tiny front garden, onto the canopy over her front door, mantle–shelfed herself up onto the window ledge and leaned in head first through her fanlight.

"Don't drop it now," she murmured to herself as she wriggled the casement latch-key into the hole. For once it turned sweetly, the large window opened smoothly and a moment later she was inside jumping down to the floor.

There was a plump envelope on her freshly made up bed and a file. The rest of her room seemed to be how she had left it, unlike the other gaunt, dishevelled and largely empty bedrooms.

For the moment she ignored everything and returned the window key to her neighbour, politely declining any help. She hauled her rucksack inside and shut the door on it's cheap, council-issue, rim-latch. The clunk reverberated through the empty house. The rest of downstairs matched the desolation upstairs; all that was left were things for which she had no use.

John had neatly boxed everything and labelled the boxes,

Rent; Gas; Electric; Rates;

Fuses and Bulbs;

Wool;

there were several more including Christmas Decorations. Rita felt wretched, he'd taken all the furniture and he knew some of it was her own. She returned to her bedroom and her envelope.

Inside was a block of cash and a letter from her stepfather.

Dear Rita,

Wednesday Night.

I'm flitting, I'm not coming back and I'll not contact you again.

I've left a new good quality set of eating irons in the knife drawer and I've put your hallmarked Silver cutlery and all your valuable furniture in storage,

"Oh!" she exclaimed: "Sorry John, I'm accusing you of stealing it."

all the documents are in the folder, it's prepaid for two years.

Best I could do.

I need to say thanks for keeping house for me so nicely since your Mum left.

And thanks for consoling me those nights, after she ran off, it was your loving care that got me through it.

I've been silly, I bought some shares for myself that I thought would go up.

It wasn't 'Insider Trading' that's illegal, but they're saying it was. They're after me, specifically out to get me. I don't think they can prove criminal intent in court, somebody would have to lie. But having seen the lengths some supposedly upright citizens are prepared to go to, it might be too close to call and I'm not going to risk it.
I've decided to go, ex-coppers fare badly inside.
Provided they can't find me too easily, I think they'll not try too hard, just let me go. So please don't follow, it'll help them find me, and I'd rather die.
Sorry for forcing myself on you, thank you for being so nice about it. I've left you what ready cash I can lay hands on and there's gas and electric in the meter, enough for a week or so anyway and some makings. There's a Chinese in the freezer specially for you coming home. I told Mrs Scroggins that I've terminated the tenancy and handed the keys in, I haven't. The keys are in the back door, yours as well. Don't forget to hand them in when you go. The rent's paid until the end of the month, but the rumour is I'm to be arrested on Friday, so I've got to go now, remember me with kindness if you can, I'll remember you with
Love,
John.

You didn't force yourself onto me, thought Rita disconsolately as she sorted through the fat block of banknotes: *Quite the reverse. But Sod It! Just when I was getting it back together! Why is it everybody I love runs away from me? What's wrong with me?*

August 1984: Rita

Rita spent the next few days looking for an old acquaintance and between times ruthlessly sorting her clothes and belongings into those she was keeping, a large holdall full, and those she was discarding.

She eventually found Junty selling his magazines on a busy street corner.

"Fancy a lodger?"

"There's enough room in my sleeping bag, but I warn you that that plump little bum of yours is just too nice to ignore. It would be too easy to pretend you're not the wrong sex."

"Oh! That wouldn't be a major problem. It's just, could we take it steady? I've never had it up--"

"Up! Up! Nobody said anything about up! You're a girl, how awful, ugh! No dearie not up. But I'd be frotting it every morning."

"Oh frottage would be okay. I think I'd quite like that."

"Have you thought about money?"

"All girl's have the usual assets. I've been tacitly being paid for it. For a couple of years. Just never been paid for it up front before."

"You can fill shelves at the supermarket, I'm not pimping for you."

"I'll have to do it for myself then."

Junty threw his hands up in horror,

"Never without a condom!"

"Okay."

"So is this you knowing who you are, or are you still looking?"

"I came home at the weekend. To an empty house. John's done a runner. Went back to square one."

"Oh, Rita, I'm so sorry." He cuddled her head clucking over her like a mother hen. "The day might come when I leave. If that happens, I'm not running away from you, but to a new life. You can come home with me if you understand that."

"Okay. I promise when you go, I'll not say you ran away from me."

Down at the Bus Station, Rue-Rouge, she sought out the other girl that she knew about that was fending for herself and doing it successfully.

"Hi, Samantha. I've been cut loose. It's a long story. I've got a place to stay, but I need readies. Is there a pitch somewhere? Where the local girls won't get in an uproar?"

"Have you thought this through, carefully?"

Rita nodded sadly,

"Yeah."

"Come along to the café, I'll introduce you."

* * *

"Girls, this is --"

"Poppy."

"Poppy's temporarily fallen on hard times. She's a good kid; she'll pay her way. Could you just help keep her out of trouble, until she learns how to spot a gook."

"Hi. I'm Gillian. I could do with a hand tonight, if you don't mind girls. It's a bunch of stable-lads. They've had two winners and want to celebrate, but I've only just found out two of them are girls. I do girls, but only when I have to."

"I don't mind girls. Never thought about it. Just assumed all the clients would be men. But girls are okay. What will they do to me?"

"Mostly have you frig them off while they munch your tit. Occasionally other things, hump your thigh."

"I'm Sue, the Navy's in tomorrow night, we'll all be needed down in the clubs on the Quayside. Keep the punters happy. We'll take you, introduce you to the bouncers, you'll be just their meat."

The girls drifted back out to the bus station as they talked.

"When we work the clubs," explained Samantha: "we pay for it by giving the bouncers freebies afterwards."

"Understood."

"If you come down and we're not here, look on the wall." She drew Rita aside into the narrow cut through from Highgate Street. There were traces of school chalk on the wall. "Numbers of suspicious cars, anything suspicious, put it here. If it says 'Take care,' go straight home. There will be a problem, possibly a raid, or agent provocateur working."

"A lot of work comes in down the telephone." Jingle tapped the box significantly: "But always let it ring four times, because we use it too. If it rings twice, stops and then rings again, it's one of us ringing a message in, alert, warning or somat." The telephone rang. Obedient to her own instruction Jingle waited until it had rung four times. "Hello." There was a pause, then she handed the receiver to Samantha: "Janice." An ancient Landrover with a leaky exhaust lumbered round the corner. "Come on Poppy, here's our rent."

It was the small hours of the morning when Poppy climbed out of the noisy truck and made her way into the squat.

Her eyes were puffy, her head was aching and she had got through a sizeable bunch of tissues, before Rita was calm enough to join Junty in his sleeping bag.

Over the next two years Poppy earned the money that allowed Rita to live comfortably, hidden from the state run services that would have taken over her life. At first, her school grades dipped alarmingly, but she quickly adjusted to the demands of her new routine and fought her way back to the top of the class.

Rita never made false claims as to how she was coping and her circumstances slowly became public knowledge, as these things do. That West Novochester had yet another under age working girl on its books raised few eyebrows, but her name joined those of Samantha and Gillian on a secret list kept by the Pastoral Staff, Pupils Known To Be At Risk.

Chapter 2

April 1985

Megan

Megan Modale kept on walking. She knew she should return home, be a good girl, moral, chaste, respectable, but she kept on walking purposefully across the fields. She'd tried the morality stance and it didn't work for her, now she'd try the opposite one.

The derelict farm came into view.

Nine-o-clock.

Many strange things happened at nine-o-clock, momentous things, like 'The Walk'.

Losing your virginity in a derelict building could qualify.

But at least I'm here through choice, she thought. *I'm not about to be raped -- Or hanged -- Hmm -- I might get hanged.*

A cigarette glowed in the half-light.

"Nicely on time." Roger said and threw the butt away. "Did you take your knickers off ready, like I told you?"

"Yes."

"Good, let's, like, get to it then."

He heaved her skirt up out of the way and pressed her up against the wall. The uneven stonework held her, her body moulding to it.

April 1985: Megan

"That's the good thing about shagging older girls, they, like, do their fair share of the undressing."

Megan shut it out, she wished neither to be reminded that she was a couple of years older, nor that she was just one of his harem, not at this moment.

"You're dry. Like, loosen up girl, think sexy." He wet his fingers and resumed his preparations, she gushed her response. "That's better."

When he mounted her he did so in smooth short stabbing thrusts. Far from hurting, they sent the girl skywards in ecstasy and earthwards in faint, the wall had to clutch at her clothes, to support her weight.

Roger had fastened himself up and lit up again, by the time Megan was back down out of orbit.

"Right, get yourself straight home girl, hot bath and a dozen turkey-basters full of hot soapy water up there. We don't want any, like, accidental pregnancies around do we. You're quite good. If you're really nice to me, do my homework and stuff, I'll do that again for you sometime."

Megan watched him go. As expected she felt used and degraded, but worst of all, she'd enjoyed it beyond her wildest fears. She came to lay a ghost and get rid of her hated virginity simultaneously and only half succeeded, and if anything, the wrong half.

The moth that flirts with the candle flame eventually gets burned.

She'd willingly thrown herself into the flame, to come out the other side, scarred but free and it hadn't worked. The next time he crooked his finger, she'd peel her knickers off and spread like a fifty pence whore, there would be nothing she could do about it.

She reached out some tissues and wiped herself down. She was a little tender, but that was all, the smoothly polished handle of her hairbrush had successfully eased her past any tearing unpleasantness, long ago.

Being one of Roger's occasional shags did have its up side. Megan had assumed that the news of her fall from chaste maiden would be being wildly embellished along the gossip hot line immediately. Instead of the expected roasting, she got silence.

Those close friends who knew she was virgin, spoke as if she still was, a condition that she was careful neither to confirm, nor deny.

Obviously Roger didn't boast about his conquests. This was an action so wildly out of character that she didn't relax about it for the entire two-year duration of their affair. She did, however, publicly champion and support those girls whose reputations were besmirched.

Typically, in the local café, a boy she'd had to head off and occasionally refuse advances from boasted,

"That Jonesie, she's easy, even I've shagged her." Megan knew the shagging claim to be true, but considered her friend generous, rather than easy, something like herself, only a bit less choosy.

"A fact you should have kept to yourself!" She snapped. She stood up and extended her claws at him, as if casting a spell. "You will meet the girl of your dreams and she will say No!" The shocked and solid silence, as she sat down again, could have been served on plates. "Of course, you can remove that spell by keeping your big mouth shut in future." The silence stretched out and out, while Megan held his eyes in a fiery stare until he looked away.

Later the same evening, but several miles west of Novochester, another family was preparing for momentous changes.

Chapter 3

April 1985 -- September 1986

Colin

"I've got to stay, somebody's got to stay."

"If you're sure you're staying, you'll need these," Mrs Cavader pushed a file and a roll of velum into her son's hand. "Guard them well, you'll make a go of it eventually, it's a good farm, but we're still going."

Colin looked up from the Mortgage Details File and glanced regretfully from his Mum to his sister,

"I know. He didn't mean it you know, it was just the drink."

His mother intervened,

"We know, but another minute and he would have done it. We can't risk it. Here's the taxi. The Farmhouse is yours, those are the deeds, only the farm is mortgaged. I love you. Bye." She grabbed the handle of the nearest case and towed it out of the door. He leaned forward into his elder sister, who reached up and hugged him.

"Thanks for protecting my honour little brother."

He retaliated by straightening up and consequently, lifting her off the ground. When he went to kiss her she smooched him, after a moment he responded by sensuously squishing her bottom.

"That's in case I never get another chance. I'd have held still for you." She released her hold and slid down his front and he let her go. "Bye."

"Bye Jane," he replied softly, as she too, grabbed a case and towed it away. "Just as well I didn't know." Then loudly: "Goodbye Mum."

They loaded up the taxi and he waved it off down the rough track. The farmhouse seemed suddenly huge, brooding and empty. He checked on his Dad, still lying sprawled, face down, across the hearthrug where he had fallen to a single left hook from his furious son. His breathing, although ragged, was comfortable, he'd do for now.

It was dark when the youngster returned from seeing to the stock and securing the outbuildings for the night. He threw a rug over the prone sleeper and went through to do his homework, and later, have some supper. His father's breathing slid from erratic to smooth and deep. Colin decided to leave him to it, he would sleep it off now.

He went up to bed and sadly surveyed the room that his mother and sister had shared ever since the accident that had confined his Dad downstairs. His sense of loss was deepened, but also strangely made bearable, by the wreckage of discarded clothes and lingering scent. He undressed, fetched a little towel from the airing cupboard, climbed into his sister's side and relived her kiss, in his head, whilst relieving himself with her perfume all around him.

Just as well I didn't know, he thought. *Else we'd have been doing this for real.* And spent into the towel, jerking and grunting.

Colin rose early the following morning and saw to the stock, then systematically searched the house for hidden alcohol, pouring away each stash he found. After the breakfast-time shift he tidied through, vacuuming around the sleeping form. The noise eventually awakened the older man.

"What time is it?"

"Half eleven."

"Shit! I feel rough," he said, lurching unsteadily to his feet, fighting gravity with one hand whilst holding his head with the other. "There's some medicine in the bureau, pour me a glass."

"Get it yourself, I've got work to do."

James Cavader raised his voice,

"Jane!"

"She's gone."

"What do you mean?"

"Mum, took her away, they've gone -- for ever, they're not coming back." Furious, although probably still unaware of the reality, his Dad grabbed at the nearest missile within reach, a candlestick from the sideboard and raised it.

"You throw that and I promise you Dad, I'll shove it up your arse. Mess up my house and I'll pen you outside with the stock."

The candlestick wavered,

"Whose house?"

"My house, Mum gave it to me, last thing before she left. You have been a guest here for twenty years, but now you're my guest. Another night like last night, could easily ensure it don't become twenty-one. I've got work to do."

"What happened last night?"

Colin left without replying and spent the day moving an electric fence and the stock it was penning and repairing a wooden one. At lunchtime he called in to The Swan for a pie and, being only fifteen, a pint of Pepsi.

"Your Mum gone then?"

"To Aunty Mavis for a few days, you know."

"Aye lad, we know."

"Listen, if Dad comes in, don't serve him. Please. If he telephones an order in, lose it, send it to the wrong farm, anything. But don't let him near any drink."

"I'll see what I can do."

"Thanks -- Is Mr. Peacock in?"

"Aye, downstairs, chatting Betty up likely."

Colin went to find his neighbour, flirting with the Landlord's wife.

"Jack, what will you give me for the Friesians?"

"All of them?"

"Yes, there's only me now, I can't milk them and everything else as well."

"I'd give you Market price lad, but I haven't anywhere to put them."

"Give me Market price and you can rent the long water meadow, Market price, for a year."

"Have you got the authority for this?"

"Sadly, yes."

When Colin got home, his father was sober, although ill, the house was still tidy and there was a meat stew of sorts, with potatoes and vegetables, in a pot on the table. During the meal, which proved far tastier than it looked, James asked again,

"What happened last night?"

"Nothing. Nothing actually happened, you were stopped."

"Did I hurt someone?"

"No. Not physically. Possibly mentally, well you hurt me for starters."

"But I was trying to harm somebody?"

"Leave it Dad, you don't want to know."

"Say sorry for me will you."

"I already did."

Father and son settled their life into a manageable pattern, with Colin tending the remaining sheep and free-range pigs, before and after school. His journey to and from the commuter train each day lay mainly across moor and farms, but not completely. He waited for a visit from the local Constabulary and waited and waited.

James lasted another six months. During that time he took care of the small flock of mixed fowl and any stock spending time in the outbuildings and kept the lower storey tidy with food ready on the table for his son coming home.

Colin was careful punctiliously to thank his disabled father for his contribution. Although James stayed off the booze, the damage had already been done; that winter's flu epidemic found him an easy target.

Colin stood at the graveside for several minutes alone, heaved a big sigh and turned away. At least his Dad had died peacefully, ignorant of the fact that, whilst in a drunken rage, he'd tried to rape his seventeen-year-old daughter, the night before she left.

Colin's letter to his sister, care of Aunty Mavis, informing her of the death, was returned a few days after the funeral, along with a note that they hadn't been gone long, but left promising to write. They had done so, but from abroad, with no permanent address. This was followed a month later by one from Jane, postmarked Chicago, Illinois.

Dear Kid Brother,

-- and I got the part. So I'll be on tour for the next two years, singing three or four nights a week. You've probably never heard of the group, but it is a highly respected Jazz Ensemble and we perform to packed houses. I'll write regularly, but don't try to write back, I'd probably never get them. There's a UK tour planned, in three or four years time, after we record the next album, (which I'm co-writing!) I'll see you then.

Mum sends her love and is thoroughly enjoying protecting me from the evils of Show Business, as my Manager.

(But, I do get away sometimes and when I do, I have been known to be very naughty! Even naughtier than I was all those years ago with Jack - -- !!) Love to you, look after Dad, I do know he didn't mean to --

When the letters questioning who was living at Vertlea began arriving, Colin filed them away, but answered none of them. He didn't volunteer times when he would be available for appointments and didn't keep the appointments made for him.

After several months of successful evasion by the young farmer, an officious junior clerk from Social Services caught up with him at home by the simple expedient of turning up mid afternoon and waiting.

"Ah, Colin Cadaver?"

"Nope!" The clerk consulted his papers.

"I thought this was Vertlea Farm."

"It's Vertlea Farm, but I'm not Colin Cadaver, you could try Low Trefoille, five miles up the valley, people often get the two villages mixed up. High Trefoille and Low Trefoille."

The clerk was back late the following day, holding something under his coat away from the elements.

"You are, Colin Cavader!"

"Yes -- did you find him?"

"Who?"

"The dead guy you were looking for yesterday." Exasperated, the clerk returned to the job in hand.

"We need to ask you some questions."

"That would be the Royal We would it?"

"What? -- I need to ask you some questions."

"Why?"

"We need some information."

"About what?"

"Your home circumstances."

"Why?"

The clerk strode over to the farmhouse door opened it and stepped into the storm porch out of the rain. He pulled out a file and opened it. He held papers up,

"Come inside and fill in this form for me."

"You have just opened my door, uninvited and entered my home. Is that breaking and entering? Or just entering? Either way it's against the law, even the Police would ask permission. You're leaving."

"I need--"

"Preferably before I have you arrested for burglary." He verified the time on his watch: "No, not quite yet, housebreaking."

"I--"

"Which wouldn't go down too well with your bosses. My guess."

The clerk left.

The following day Colin paid his solicitor a visit and subsequently his neighbour, Jack Peacock's wife, Jill.

By judiciously varying his route home, and time of arrival, he was able to give the Social the run around for the further three weeks required for him to reach sixteen.

The day following his birthday, Jill escorted him to the Social Services Office, where they presented the solicitors letter and spelled out in simple language that Colin was not to be troubled again.

"Any guidance he needs from an adult, he's getting from me. We just live two miles along the valley. You townies wouldn't understand, but to us country folk, that's not next door, it's merely downstairs."

Chapter 4

April 1986

Poppy

The Girls were in the café, sitting in the corner booth, Poppy moved over to join them. They made space for her, Samantha wasn't there, but any friend of Samantha's was okay.

The subject of the angry conversation was the brand new telephones that had been installed, that week, in the Rue-Rouge Bus Station. Poppy hadn't seen them yet, but knew the Girls were vitriolic about them.

"We need an alarm system, it's stupid these new 'phones not accepting calls, it's bad for business and it's dangerous." Gillian was furious, some of her most lucrative assignments used to come down the telephone next to the bus stop.

"They can be rigged to accept calls," The redhead behind the counter murmured into the gap behind the till: "Get Samantha to check with Timothy Ebsenter or Ben Brown, I'm sure they can, but you'd need a telephone engineer in your pocket, to do the necessary."

"Got one," said Jingle.

"And me," said Bobbie: "But I'll let Samantha check first."

The bent coin obligingly jammed in the slot just too far in to be extracted with pliers, Samantha walked round to the other telephone box and rang for maintenance. The engineer that turned up was a total stranger and female! The girls held a hurried council of war; Jingle scurried over to the newsagents and bought an ice cream. The young engineer lifted the cover off the telephone; Samantha looked inside, the PCB was one of the three kinds that she had learned how to fix, she nodded at Jingle.

"Oh no!" Jingle was holding an empty cornet. The ice cream complete with its flake was lying splattered in the telephone engineer's toolbox. Poppy moved in to help clean up the mess, then they watched as the coin was deftly removed, the electronics cleaned and the cover replaced. They could see that the young engineer was mildly annoyed, with something obviously on her mind.

"We're sorry. About messing your bag up," murmured Poppy.

"You could have just asked!"

The working girl did the sums and came up with the correct answer, the girl's glasses were huge, not just a necessity, but also a fashion statement. She decided to try the truth,

"We thought it better. That you didn't know. You wouldn't need to lie."

"You should have asked me, we would have found a way."

"We're really sorry, would you check the other one while you are here, then we can be confident that they are both working properly?"

The girl gazed silently into Samantha's eyes for a moment. She must have fully understood that this time she was 'being asked,' because she performed the task slowly and methodically, specifically not checking on what Samantha was doing. She moved her bag round into the other booth, removed the cover and laid it on the ground, then she cleaned and dusted out the inside of the case, picked the cover up and replaced it.

"Thank you," said Samantha: "If ever I can be of any service, I do girls and hen nights too and I owe you one." The engineer looked steadily at her again, then nodded at the telephone,

"Whom do I ask for?"

"Samantha." Like the engineer, the youngster nodded at the telephone: "How will you manage over their different status?"

"Nothing to do with me, I didn't actually see you change the jumper over, I can assume they had been left set up that way."

Samantha smiled gently straight into the girl's eyes,

"Thank you and we really are sorry about the bag, you don't meet that many people that you can trust in our job."

For the first time the engineer relaxed and smiled back, in complete understanding. She returned her tools to her van, but then stood vacillating.

"What do you drive, your own car?"

"Battered Landrover, with a direct-able hand light on the roof of the cab."

"I'll be watching for it, about quarter past five?"

The engineer fidgeted indecisively for a moment, but then got into her van and drove off without another word.

"How in the hot place did she know?" asked Jingle.

"The glasses, my friend Sally says if the light's right it's like looking in a mirror.

"She won't have been able to see what Samantha did." Added Poppy. "But she will have seen the movement. When Sam reached in to make the switch. The jumper was the only clean item on the board. After she switched it. Shone like a beacon. She'll have known instantly."

* * *

"Here's your Landrover, Sam," called Jingle quietly. The vehicle approached hesitantly; regular punters knew not to do that. They drove straight up to their target girl briskly.

"She'll be done for curb crawling, if she's not careful," said the tiny working girl and stepped out to the edge of the pavement. The Landrover stopped and she got in,

"I just came to tell-"

"Drive girl, you gotta drive away. Now!" Partly in shock, partly in natural obedience the telephone engineer drove away.

"She'd bottled it," said Poppy.

Jingle agreed,

"Yeah, but Sam'll sort her out, make it worth her while."

* * *

During their coffee break in the café Samantha went fishing.

"I've got a mildly-submissive lesbian-bondage client who wants a long term partner, anyone know of anybody looking? Somebody nice."

"Not mine." replied Poppy: "They're all not somebody nice."

"I thought of taking her to de Voyage on Tuesday, to see if we could spot something suitable."

"Give Jonja a ring," suggested Jingle: "See if her crew are going on Tuesday, there's a couple of her mates that could measure up. Gosbury prefix, thirty-eight twenty-seven."

Back out on the street, Samantha crossed over to the telephone and dialled the unfamiliar number carefully,

"Can I speak to Jonja please?" The rest of the discourse was lost as the schoolgirl buried her head deep in the hood, away from the traffic noise.

"Who is it?" asked Poppy.

"It'll be that telephone engineer, she's lovely, I wouldn't mind a go myself."

"You're straight!"

"That's a measure of how lovely she is!"

"All fixed," said Samantha, as she rejoined the group: "Jonja's going on Tuesday, she'll aim us in the right direction.

On Tuesday night the young engineer walked confidently straight up to the girls and greeted them.

"Hi everyone." She lifted her eyebrows at Samantha.

"Have you any prejudices; Jews, Asians, Martians? I'm not looking to challenge your views just to avoid problems."

"None that I'm aware of, not in the way you mean. When I described de Voyage's bouncers as gorillas, I wasn't being racist, the two most fear inspiring were white lads. I don't like loud, or smelly, pointless bravado or vandalism. I had a very old copy of 'Beauty and the Beast' as a kid. I loved that Beast, the story was true to its roots, you know the Beast being beautiful inside?" Samantha nodded.

"I tossed myself silly over the picture where the Beast gave Beauty her rose."

"So if a Martian was nice, it wouldn't matter what colour she was?"

"No."

"That's OK then, I've set up a meet in de Voyage with a regular who knows lots of girls. She answers to Jonja."

"Like I answer to Shannon?"

"Yeah. She could possibly point us in the right direction. She's not from Mars, somewhere much closer and much hotter, Equatorial Africa."

"Oh, she's not circumcised is she?" Shannon's voice was full of concern.

"I don't know. My guess is not, but I don't know. Would it be a problem?"

"Not for me, but tragic for her, she would have no feeling, she wouldn't be able to come."

"Let's hope not then. But, there's a problem, I can't make it, could Poppy take you?"

Shannon turned her dazzling smile on the other girl.

"Sure."

Shannon walked up to the door with Poppy on her arm as if she had been doing it all her life.

"Hello Poppy," said the human mountain guarding the door, with a big smile. The grizzled Silverback was obviously greeting an old friend.

"Hi Barney, Shannon wants a single night membership." The bouncer opened the door, waved them through and directed the girls over towards reception.

"Thank you Barney." They said in unison.

"Have a lovely evening Shannon."

The girls joined the short queue at reception and when her turn came Shannon placed three £10 notes on the counter,

"Poppy and a single night membership for Shannon." The receptionist issued the girls with the cards, with their two tear off portions for their free drinks. Poppy clenched her left hand into a fist and allowed the girl to stamp it on the back. Shannon copied her exactly.

Jonja was easily identified; the big Negress was looking out for them, picked them out of the throng immediately and came over, confidently.

"You must be Poppy."

"Yep. Jonja, this kid's not called Shannon. Shannon, this one's not called Jonja."

"Hi Shannon."

"Hi Jonja."

"Care to dance?"

"Yes Please."

"See you around, Poppy, I'll take it from here."

"Goodnight, Poppy and thank you, thank Samantha for me too please." Shannon flowed into the embrace, bonding herself to the front of the taller girl all the way down.

Not already surely, thought Poppy, *I haven't in all honesty earned my fee yet!* But she had, the girls hadn't danced together for two minutes when Shannon laughed for the first time and Jonja grinned at her reply.

Potentially that was another satisfied customer.

The working girl headed for the door and her nights work. Before she left she carefully checked the date on the back of her hand under the UV lamp. You never knew which ship was anchored round the bend and if another client later that evening wanted to bring her back here, there was no need and every reason not, to make her pay twice.

Back at the bus stop at Rue Rouge, all the girls had gone.

A car drew up; Poppy hurried up the street to greet the new punter,

"Looking for business pet?" She called as she approached.

The driver was middle aged and unsure.

"Erm -- I'm not sure duck, what are you offering?"

He was a tourist up from Yorkshire way, or businessman with a night free of appointments.

"Twenty for in the car. Or a hundred all night in your hotel."

"Would that be with --"

"I'm condom only. I never do it without."

"So that's twenty pounds for full sex in the car?"

"Or the full night--" The man relaxed back. Too late the warning hairs on the back of her neck went right up. Poppy whirled round. Reaching for her were two big men with huge feet. Between them, chalked on the wall, just inside the entrance to the cut through, she could just see the words,

Take Care.

At the Police Station, Sergeant Josephine Fairchild and Sergeant Elaine Jacques processed Poppy.

"I'm Rita Roundheels, I'm eighteen years old. Date of birth, seven, nine, sixty-seven. I live in a squat down Ryker way."

"Professional name?"

"Poppy."

"Who's your pimp?"

"I'm freelance."

"Are you on drugs?"

Rita rolled up her sleeves,

"No. Never touch the stuff."

"Would you be prepared to be breathalysed?"

"Breath, Blood or Urine tested. Never touch the stuff. Mugs game."

"Is there anyone who could vouch for you?"

"Samantha."

"Samantha who?"

"Samantha Hutt."

"How are you going to plead?"

"I'll plead guilty to soliciting. I was, I can't deny it, I'm not a liar!"

Sergeant Fairchild left them for a few minutes.

"Get a good solicitor kid, but don't change your plea. If you don't muck us about we will try to look after you." Elaine drew Poppy away into the corridor and whispered close to her ear. "Is that your real name?"

Astonished the girl gasped out,

"Yes."

"Despite your claim that you don't lie, I know it's not your real age, is it your real name?" This time the answer was much more controlled,

"Oh, yes. The name's mine right enough. I might fudge my age, but I wouldn't lie, not -- not **lie**." The other girl nodded in understanding.

When Sergeant Fairchild returned she just thrust Poppy's statement under her nose and said,

"Sign here."

The good solicitor pleaded for mitigation, first offence and any other wriggle she could think of and Poppy got off with a hundred pound fine and two years probation. She also stayed out of the clutches of the Social Services.

The criminal record she gained for committing a crime that is one of the least understandable anomalies of justice systems in most parts of the World was to prove costly later.

Chapter 5

April 1986

Sebastian

Sebastian Stripe plodded down the hill, towards his back yard door. He avoided the narrow pavement, choosing to walk in the gutter, rather than risk scraping his clothes on the grime encrusted walls that towered over him either side of the steep back lane.

Far below, he could see the armament works and beyond that the flat, slack, black-expanse of the Tyne. The still, silent-strip was bordered on both sides by mud banks. Straining hard, he imagined that he could just see the sprinkling of wading birds that came and went with low tide fastidiously selecting succulent morsels from the packed larder beneath their feet.

He lifted the sneck on his back door, entered and stopped abruptly, face to billow with a wet towel.

Shit! It rained yesterday didn't it! Silent and furtive now, cursing himself for his poor memory, he closed the door and picked his way through the washing-festooned back yard and climbed the back stairs wearily. It wasn't sufficient that he had three new homeworks for tomorrow and two more he should have done last week, but in addition it was Tuesday, read Washing-Day-If-Monday's-Wet, as well. He dearly wished he could adopt his Dad's strategy. At the first glimpse of a line being strung across the yard, a mere wisp of steam on the air and Seb Stripe Senior did a sharp about turn and tiptoed away to the pub, or, more often these days since she got her own place, Maud's little flat. Likewise the two younger boys always managed to have seriously time consuming weekly assignations, elsewhere, every Washday.

"-- no consideration, leaving things in pockets and he'll argue he doesn't. I'll give him what for when he comes in."

So today it was something in his pockets, last week it was his socks rolled up, next week it might be that they were too dirty; he stifled a presence-betraying sigh.

If only his Mum was more like her Sister. Nothing was too much trouble for Maud, he only called her Aunt in his mother's presence, she'd specifically asked him not to otherwise. Maud loved him unconditionally. It was she who'd held his sobbing face to her bosom, the day he'd been bullied at school over the skid-marks on his underpants and advised him on cleanliness and more frequent changes of clothing. The tormenting by his classmates and thrashing from his mother had almost been worth it, for the voluptuous eroticism of the contact with his young aunt's breasts, bra-less inside her thin dress. She hadn't even pulled away from his furtively groping hand, unaware of his touch, or, a circumstance he thought less likely, making a superb pretence that she was.

The boy removed his shoes and sat on the stairs until the grumbling voice receded. Then he slipped quietly into and out of the kitchen, up the uncarpeted back stairs. The chances were that he'd still get a hiding later, but at least he'd be able to sit and do his homework now, rather than having to stand.

He managed two of the new homeworks, but then spent an hour on the third, ending up with the same wrong answer that he'd got after five minutes. With a sigh he turned his attention to the outstanding ones that had already taken him several hours last week and spent the rest of the evening getting no further, despite trying so hard it almost hurt.

Sebastian's abysmal success rate, in his own eyes, as a son and indifferent performance in his homework, was matched by, or if anything, exceeded in failure, where relations with the opposite sex were concerned.

A typical encounter occurred the following day.

Seb was the first of his group to arrive at school and he watched as two younger girls approached. Despite being slightly hampered by her friend the blonde one asked,

"Are you, Colin?"

"No silly, I told you. He's not, Colin!" The tall one had pre-empted any reply.

"What do you want Colin for?"

"My mate wants to go out with him," replied the blonde.

"No she doesn't, I'll go out with her."

"Not you, she wants, Colin."

"No she doesn't, she wants me. Tell her I'll go out with her."

"She wants, Colin, I don't know anyone who wants to go out with you."

The taller girls ill concealed scorn produced an automatic response,

"Oh well bugger off then!"

* * *

The following Sunday, the Stripe boys, as usual, were sent out for a walk in the morning.

"Be back for eleven, for Sunday school."

Seb didn't reply.

Just why his parents sent their children to the local church Sunday school, when they went nowhere near the place themselves was a mystery and a source of resentment. The strange omission of failing to provide him with some kind of watch before imposing a timetable upon him was equally incomprehensible, but allowed Seb to lose track of time and miss the hated appointment most weeks. The day was warm, the Dene deserted and his kid brothers for once, well behaved. They worked their way along the bed of the dry valley, turning over stones looking for wildlife. The river now ran in a pipe, several metres underground, the boys had almost forgotten it was Sunday by the time--

"Seb! What are you playing at?" Seb Stripe Senior's voice, calling from the top of the slope, caught them chasing a mouse in the long grass and ensured its escape.

"Nothing. I'm not playing at nothing."

"It's after twelve-o-clock. You were told to be back --" The severe dressing down from his Dad was accepted without any of the usual demur that would be served up to anyone else.

Seb Senior didn't take backchat.

And anyway he was usually right. Besides, the telling off was the price to avoid a beating from his Mum, both of which gave precedence to Sunday school in the hate stakes.

The other source of beatings took place annually, Parent's Day at school. Every year certain teachers told Mrs Stripe that her son was boisterous, wilful and didn't work hard enough. Others maintained that if given firm guidance, he was an able student who worked well. The irony of the situation was that Sebastian always worked hard, but only some of this effort had any effect. Often he would snatch at the work, misunderstand and answer the wrong question, or, even when he understood, he might answer in the wrong way. Many teachers were unaware of the hours he toiled, taking a poorly presented piece of indifferent-work to be proof of no effort. By the time Mrs Stripe got home, consumed with the desire for revenge, any positive assessments had long been forgotten. Parental guidance about how to work steadily all year, checking of homework, general encouragement and attempts to facilitate a better performance next year, were not only not forthcoming, they were never thought about.

Every year he expected hidings, got them, cried and then, treating it as just a fact of life, forgot about it, unaware that the unjust treatment was leaving its invisible, but nonetheless indelible mark.

Chapter 6

April 1986

Roger

On the edge of town, Roger Redcombe lay in the rough grass, between the derelict farm buildings, pulling the last leg off a harvestman. After a moment he squashed it, they were no fun when the legs ran out and looked round for something else to alleviate his boredom. If he wasn't careful he'd end up doing his homework himself, just for something to do, but at that moment an older girl walked round the corner.

"Meg," he called. "In here." The girl looked around her for eavesdroppers, then called softly,

"I've still got my school regs on."

"Come and give uz a suck." The girl joined him kneeling in the rough grass, whilst popping buttons on her blouse. Roger reached in, heaved a breast out and began suckling her roughly.

"Careful, don't tear it." He eased his caveman approach a bit, pummelling her tit as he sucked. When she began tenderly to caress his hair, he stopped.

"Take my bag with you, do my homework for me and I'll, like, give you a nice shagging later." The girl watched him stuff her glistening breast back into her top.

"You're a right bastard, you are."

"But I'm good in bed. Nine-o-clock and I'll, like, make it worth your while."

Obviously resigned to the situation, but by no means best pleased, Megan shouldered his bag,

"Yes you are good in bed, but you're still a dangerous bastard!"

"And the two together you find, like, irresistible."

Scowling, Megan left to do her work and his.

It was quarter past nine when Roger found her waiting for him, in the derelict building. As usual when he was late, her hand was up her skirt, this time she didn't even bother to remove it, but kept on stroking herself.

"You said nine-o-clock."

"Like, I've been busy, are you ready?"

"Busy keeping me waiting. You bastard."

He pressed her against the wall and felt up her skirt, she was hot and wet, ready.

"That's a good girl, like, nicely ready, come to Daddy and get done." She grunted softly and slumped as he sank up her. Her head jerked rhythmically in time with his thrusting; her half open eyes were glazed and unseeing.

Chapter 7

April 1986

Poppy

The squat was deserted, but clean and tidy. Junty had spent at least part of the day on housework, but he wasn't around. Rita munched the supermarket, cardboard-in-carpet-tiles sandwich that she'd brought in with her, while she did some of her homework. When it got too dark to write, she lit the hurricane lamp, peeled her school uniform off, right down to skin and dressed herself in a short, tight, elasticised skirt, a tight top, hold-ups and boots. She broke open a new gross box of condoms, selected a shoulder bag from several lying beside an enormous sleeping bag and stuffed several hands-full of packs of three into it. Finally she inspected the product in her hand mirror.

"Yes girl, whoever you are, you'll have to do. Let's go and earn some rent."

The small, exclusive club was tucked away down an alley; the bouncers on the door welcomed her with genuine smiles,

"Hello, Poppy, we were hoping to see you, we're really in the mood tonight."

"Well let's hope I'm in demand then."

"Oh you will be, there's several of your regulars in and several on the lookout."

"Okay. See you later boys."

The girl was guided in, ahead of a slowly moving queue, with a familiar, friendly and gentle, smack on the bottom.

A number of girls spent some time, far from alone, in the ladies toilet cubicles that night. The main difference between Poppy and the rest of them being most of them made only one visit and squealed breathily; Poppy made several and did so mainly in silence, although her partners frequently grunted in a satisfied manner, or, in the case of the two female clients, squealed.

And, of course, Poppy got paid.

When the club closed, she joined the bouncers in their room and paid her dues, while they played pass the parcel, until no-one could get hard again, whereupon they sent her home in a taxi. The taxi driver was horrified at the location,

"Is this right Miss?"

"Yeah, this is home. Is that it, on the meter?"

"Yes."

"Can I fuck you for it?"

"The money please Miss. The other's very tempting, but I'm married."

"Here you are then. Keep the change."

"Thank you Miss." Poppy dived out of the taxi and into the squat. Only a few seconds later Rita climbed into her tracksuit, slid into Junty's big double sleeping bag beside him and crashed out.

The little alarm clock woke her and she killed the sound, but lay still, waiting. Junty was energetically having her bottom, through his and her tracksuit; so his systematic quartering of the city's business sector the previous night had most probably been in vain. Presently the grunting activity slowed and stopped.

"Thanks." he said.

"Finished?"

"Yes -- Thanks."

"Who am I? Don't tell me you've forgotten already."

"Thanks Frank."

"That's better." She got up to finish her homework, while Junty resurrected the fire and rustled up some breakfast.

"We need some stores," he said: "And I've had a bad week."

She waved at her shoulder bag and he brought it across.

"I don't go into girls handbags. I'd hate it if I found some ugly old queen rummaging through mine."

She grinned as she pulled last night's roll of notes out and handed it over. He peeled off a couple of big ones and handed the rest back and Rita resumed her work.

Only a few minutes later her view of it was rudely interrupted by a tray carrying a fried egg breakfast, toast, butter, marmalade and black coffee.

"You will make him a very good wife."

"Chance would be a fine thing. You know what, I'll tell him if I ever see him again."

Rita got dressed for school in clean knickers, but otherwise the same school clothes as the previous day. She paused for a moment to let Junty kiss her goodbye, between shaving and putting his face on, collected up all her personal belongings into her school-bag and paused again at the door. Her squat-mate primped in the mirror then turned to her for inspection. Despite never making any attempt to disguise his sex, he was just about the prettiest person she knew and one of the nicest.

"You're nice. A good cook and a seriously good housekeeper. He'd be totally mad to pass you up. And you're pretty too."

"Ooh! Get her!"

"Bye nutcase."

"Bye dearie. If you see him, tell him."

Rita left grinning and called into the Left Luggage office of the station on her way to school. The regular porter was on duty and she merely waved at him as she approached. The door clicked open and she was left alone to burrow through to the back and exchange several items between her school bag and the big holdall, that had been a fixture on its shelf for two years.

Chapter 8

April 1986

Mary

The bullying shouts rang out clearly.

Mary Andrew ducked her head and scurried after her Gran. Despite the old lady's diminutive size and her own development being at the leggy stage, she found it difficult to keep up.

"Frumpy, Mary! Mary long frock!"

Again, Mary gave no sign of having heard the taunts hurled at her from across the park.

"Keep up girl. We mustn't be late." The gap in front of her widened and Mary kicked even harder to compensate. The Rectory came into view around the corner. Soon she would be safely out of sight among the dark corridors, smelling of cold and old polish.

Now remember, thought Mary, *children--*

"Now remember, children should be seen and not heard."

"Yes Gran."

Gran knocked and let them into the kitchen.

"Hello." Cook was busy in the kitchen and greeted them warmly. Mary liked the rotund little woman. Although she reiterated her instructions as often as all the other adults in her life, she did so from the viewpoint that you were obeying them, rather than assuming that you weren't.

"Do you want a cuppa before you start?"

"No," said Gran, despite the question having been aimed mainly at Mary. "We'll just get on."

Mary gave Cook a little smile and hurried through to the Library, freedom and to wait. She didn't have to wait long. Cook bustled in carrying a small tray, with a mug of tea. There were also two scones on a plate. A thick pat of melting butter was oozing from the centre of the nearer one.

"I'll just put these here to cool, they might disappear with a bit of luck, then I can wash the crocks," she said, laid the tray down and left.

Mary cooled the scones and tea to blood heat, in her stomach.

The quality was well up to Cook's usual cordon bleu standard.

The youngster pulled on the polish-stained working-gloves, restricting herself to only one further longing glance towards the end of the table and surveyed her task. She was working through one whole shelf of books at a time. Told only to clean and polish them, but above all, not get them mixed up, she'd quickly perfected an efficient routine. Transfer the books from shelf to table, dusting them as she did so. Dust the shelf. Lovingly polish the exquisite leather covers and return each book in sequence. The boring, mindless-task was a perfect foil to the harsh realities of her life outside.

The main responsibility for the name-calling, and occasionally worse, was having to wear a succession of cast-offs from the Charity Shop, chosen for her by her Gran, apparently primarily for their high frump index. Most of the girls at school refrained from even being friendly with Frumpy Mary Long Frock, never mind letting her into their inner circle.

Helping Gran clean the rectory pushed the unpleasantness out of focus for a while and brought with it two bonuses.

She glanced again at the first, a huge tome lying open at the end of the table. Her white gloves lay upon it waiting for lunch time, when she could read the next exciting instalment of her adventures in the Wild West,

Or, today, she silently reminded herself, *I'll re-read, re-live the last one.*

Her mind drifted off, two centuries ago and thousands of miles westwards. Her thoughts racing through the story-so-far, to get to the juicy bit --

Homeless orphan, Mary Richards, had worked and skivvied, scrimped and saved to buy her stage-coach-ticket out to the new frontier. Her change of clothes and other few possessions were in a tiny box strapped to the boot.

The child reading the story had appreciated the magnitude of the trip. Whilst not quite Neil Armstrong, for an unescorted teen-aged girl it was certainly a Nineteenth Century equivalent to Ed White's Space Walk, with a similar abrupt and tragic end to her career hovering in the wings, a distinct possibility[2]. Consequently she had been as nervous and excited as the heroine the whole time, and reading the current part of the story, quite scared.

The sixteen-year-old in the story and the not quite fourteen-year-old reading it merged personalities seamlessly.

They were travelling through Indian Territory and the news had not been good at the last town. There had been rumours of incidents and the local ranchers had advised them not to go.

The local Coach Company Representative, however, whose job was also on the line, had ordered the driver out, on pain of dismissal.

The residents called their settlement a town, but Mary hadn't registered it as such. In fairness it was the largest place they had called at for the last two hundred miles. Half of the buildings had two storeys and the other three still had proper boardwalks outside them.

---

[2] Lt Col Edward Higgins White II: first American to Walk In Space on June 3, 1965. Less than two years later he, along with Virgil Grissom and Roger Chaffee, died in the fire during a launch rehearsal, on board the designated Apollo 1. The Investigations into the fire resulted in major changes in the cockpit design and launch procedure.

April 1986: Mary

In the livery stable, the hayloft above the horses had been warm and dry and nobody had seen her quickly climb the ladder. As darkness fell, and apart from the horses, the building became deserted, the young woman had been able to come out from her hiding place and savour her day's meagre ration of food, by eating it very slowly, with lots of water. She revelled in the luxury of being able to strip off and air her clothes, while she slept soundly, wrapped only in her cloak. Early the following morning, the huge animals with their large limpid eyes had not objected when she stole some more of their drinking water, to bathe herself for the first time for more than a week.

Trembling and fearful, but determined to make it, the occupants of the coach-and-six set off to dash to the next staging post.

They ran into the ambush not quite half way there.

The first wave of arrows had wounded the driver and taken out the guard.

Mary, travelling as baggage on top, had grabbed his rifle and sold her life dearly, as brave after brave fell to her fire.

The rifle was almost too hot to hold, when she ran out of ammunition.

She scrabbled around the dead guard's person, looking for some more.

There was a searing pain at the back of her head; a bright flash of light and then everything went black.

"Hello, Mary."

She jerked. The smell of gun-smoke faded. The hot, dust-laden air cooled and cleared. Nearly all the books had been polished and replaced by her willing hands, as her brain drifted in fantasy.

"Oh hello Curate. I - was --"

"Call me Nigel when we are alone, I've told you." Mary gave him her little smile but said nothing. The Curate sat down in an easy chair and held his hands out. She walked over to him, to enjoy the other bonus. For a child short on cuddles, Nigel was Heaven sent. He turned her round, as always and lifted her backwards into his lap. He wriggled against her and hugged her tight and told her stories about scullery maids who fell in love with Princes and lived happily ever after.

The cuddles got tighter and tighter, as the wriggling got stronger and Mary lived the story more and more personally.

There were times that she could hardly breathe, he squeezed her so tightly and panted and grunted, but Mary didn't mind. The Prince loved his scullery maid and rode off with her into the sunset --

"Was that a nice story?"

"Yes. Lovely. Thank you."

"You best finish your books. Then come straight down, lunch is nearly ready."

She gave him the little smile, as she climbed off him and began polishing again as he left the library.

Lunch was English cooking at its best in the Rectory kitchen, it was tasty and there was enough of it.

"I'm going to read my book until two. Then I'll do another shelf." Grandma didn't reply, but Cook asked, as always,

"You are wearing the gloves aren't you?"

"Yes. One pair to polish, but the white ones to read."

Mary had barely donned the white gloves when the vicar entered,

"What are you doing?"

She completed the turn airborne,

"I was just r-r-reading t-t-this B-B-Boy's Adventure Stories b-b-book."

"Sorry, I didn't mean to startle you, I know that. Why are you wearing gloves?"

"C-C-Cook said I always had to wear gloves, to r-r-read your b-b-books."

"My books yes. My first editions, but that's just an old set of boys stories my Granddad had bound to match the rest. You can read that, you can do anything with that. It's to be thrown out."

"Oh. That's sad. They're lovely stories."

"Boys stories, I'm surprised you want to read them."

"This ones about a girl, travelling across America, just after the War of Independence. But some of the pages are torn, with bits missing. I didn't--"

"I know you didn't tear them, nor did I. I said it was to be thrown out, that's why. I'd give it to you, but it's not worth anything damaged."

"It's still readable, that's all I want."

"Oh, well take it then."

The prospect of owning such a treasure had never been considered, now it assumed the gestalt of a lottery win.

"Oh! Thank you. Thank you so much."

Back home, Mary washed up after tea,

"I'm going to bed now Gran, I'm going to read my book for a while."

"Don't read for long. Ruins your eyes, that reading stuff."

"'Night Gran."

The old lady pouted her cheek to be kissed but otherwise ignored the child. Mary, unaware that coldness between family members was unusual, kissed her and went to bed.

She opened the book, fastidiously wearing her own gloves and propped it up on her pillow. She settled herself, kneeling in the middle of the bed, in comfortable reading distance, reached for Teddy and stuffed him between her thighs, like a little horse. Then she gently rode him while she read, just like Nigel wriggled against her as he told her stories.

Again she scanned quickly through Mary Richards' night in the stables and her gunfight lying prone on top of the wildly-bucking coach, until she was taken out from behind.

Consciousness returned slowly and painfully, Mary managed neither to groan nor obviously move as she took her weight on her legs, rather than her back, which was pressed hard up against a tree. Apart from taking her weight, she couldn't move her legs and she couldn't move her arms at all. She could hear them close by, but she didn't want to alert them to the fact that she had woken up, so it took her several minutes to work out that she was tied to the tree and a glance trough slitted eyes to confirm why she was so cold.

Through the still slitted eyes, she watched them trying on her clothes, and apart from the cloak, throwing them onto the fire because they were too small. It didn't matter; she would never need them again. There were only three of them. She must have killed the rest. The pain in her head was bad, but she mustn't show it. It was only a taste of what was to come. Her arms were threatening to cramp, the tree trunk between her elbows must be quite wide. Her hands, lashed together, were only just touching on the far side of it.

Mary surreptitiously tried the bonds again, but it was useless. Indians tied their houses together, they were good with knots.

The reader rode her bear faster, it was even more exciting doing it whilst reading the actual story, rather than remembering it. She could smell the wood-smoke and feel the rough bark cutting into her naked back.

She rode the bear intimately -- more and more intimately.

The tall one said something and they all looked at her and laughed. They'd realised she was awake. The three men turned towards her and shed the few clothes they were wearing.

It was time.

Mary stood with head hung submissively, wondering if they would release her before they started, that way, she could go down fighting to the end. If not, they would be able to do anything they liked to her, while she would have to meekly stand there and let them.

Mary Andrew grunted and fell over as the feeling washed through her, her squashing thighs and thrusting hips driving the little bear on to greater pinnacles of achievement. Presently she slowed down and stopped, there was cleaning up to do and her lovely storybook to put away until tomorrow.

April 1986: Mary

She had no worries for her heroine; fictitious, Mary Richards was safe.

She knew that the following sentence read,

A man rose in front of her, apparently out of the bare ground and gunned down the three braves advancing towards her.

But in her mind, while riding her bear, he rescued her the morning after, not the night before.

Chapter 9

April 1986

Ben

Benjamin Brown went home from school confused. He was sure he was straight, but the Head of English had tricked him into being alone with him in the stock cupboard, bent him over his knee and spanked him and caressed his buttocks sensuously between spanks. The spanks hadn't hurt and the caresses had been nice. Nice enough to cause him to have an erection, which he'd had difficulty hiding. He'd then had to face the teasing, 'Boris's Bum Boy,' with the associated pointing fingers, when he returned to the classroom. Furious, he suspected he'd been guilty of protesting too much.

He stopped off at the derelict farm, hoping to catch sight of one of the local youths shagging a girl. In the past he'd seen several, and been really surprised at which girls shagged, not to mention how willingly they did it.

Redcombe was there, the give-away hair, several decades out of fashion, was just visible in the long grass. Ben crept closer, silently. The swarthy boy usually provided good action for voyeurs, but would have killed Ben, if he ever suspected him of spying on him.

A youngster who lived in the next street walked by, her well filled top at variance with the plaits betraying her true age. In a couple of years she'd be really serious crumpet. Apparently, Roger thought she already merited his attention and called to her, with an invitation as loud as it was explicit. Without turning her head, the girl politely declined and walked on completely ignoring the hard crust of a cow pat that he frisbeed past her head in his fury at being rejected.

Nothing happened for several minutes and Ben was just about to slip away when Megan appeared.

For several weeks, Ben relived the sight of Megan's tit being eaten, but with himself doing the eating.

Would she hold still for me just to heave one out and munch on it? He thought. He hadn't realised how terrific his lovely next-door neighbour's breasts were, well the left one anyway, but the hurried glimpses he'd had, generated many fanciful flights where he became better acquainted with them. Realistic strategies, detailing exactly how he was to achieve this in real life, he carefully didn't consider. In his own eyes Megan was out-of-his-league.

In Assembly a few days later the Fourth Year were introduced to the imminent arrival of Work Experience, where they would have the opportunity, for a week, of testing jobs out for suitability.

A few days after that, during a Careers lesson, their Year Tutor stressed that there was no need to strive for their planned chosen career, if it were unlikely they would get a placement.

"For example, Nursing is out, the health of the General Public cannot be put at risk in the hands of a clueless fifteen year old. However being a shop assistant in a busy shop is very similar as far as being a thankless drudge is concerned. Sore swollen feet. Running here, running there, carrying heavy loads. Stroppy members of the public blaming you for their mistakes. Telling you, you're a total cretin. If you fail to cope with that and rise above it, you'll never make a nurse."

Roger's muttered comment was both derogatory and grossly impolite.

Mr Baques waded over to his desk through the ensuing silence, spun a chair round and sat forked across it facing him.

"You have every right to challenge that statement Roger, but not to be rude. You will pay for the rudeness by justifying your question, which, minus the Anglo-Saxon was 'What does he know about work?' I believe."

There was silence. Up close and personal, Stewart Baques' baby blue eyes glinted dangerously. Roger visibly shrank away from such a head on challenge.

"What branch of the World of Work would you like me to give you my experience of? Farming? Engineering? What?"

Roger twitched uncomfortably,

"Transport? Commerce? Building?"

"Have you done all those?" Ben asked.

"All those and more, although naturally I would have to sit at Colin's feet and listen, if he chose to talk about farming. Or Rita's if she wanted to give us tips about survival in a hostile world." He continued to look straight into Roger's eyes. "I know when I'm overmatched."

"Sorry," murmured the boy.

"Is there a heading you would like me to enlarge on?" His voice was no longer jagged, but gentle, supportive, street-cred restoring.

Roger shook his head but Seb called,

"Transport."

"Transport. The Railway. Carriage Service on British Rail was a choice between the pits and the skive! The pits was cleaning, cleaners are dreadfully paid and it's a filthy, soul destroying job, the skive was filling the carriages with water."

"Didn't the passengers object?" asked Colin, precipitating a round of laughter.

"Frequently, so we filled the toilet cisterns instead. Next time you see an old British Rail Inter City train, look at the end of the carriage, there will be a pipe down, that's the pipe for filling the water tanks. When The Flying Scotsman or other Inter-City trains were due, we would go down onto the track and wait. The Scotsman only stopped for four minutes." Ben thought it through quickly.

"That's not long."

"Not long enough, bearing in mind that it was at the only stop between Edinburgh and Kings Cross! There were about half a dozen of us, two or three carriages each, we had to shove a hose on a pipe and turn it on, then run to the next." Whilst speaking, Mr Baques had returned to the front of the class and performed an exaggerated, 'get those knees up' run, illustrating his narrative, most of the class giggled. "Shove that pipe on and open the valve, run to the next. You could get four on if you were really slick. Then you heard the guard's whistle blow. Close the valve, yank the first off, run, close the second, yank it off, run, by now the train was moving, run faster. All along the train hose pipes were stretching out, still filling the water tanks, eventually they could stretch no more and binged off, I'd love to say water flew everywhere. You know 'Passengers as far away as Peterborough getting P-wet'." Again the class obligingly giggled: "But it didn't, the water was flowing fast enough, but at low pressure."

"Why was it a skive?" asked Ben again.

"It might be two hours to the next train, but we were 'Carriage Service', couldn't do anything else, demarcation."

There was an enlightened murmur throughout the room.

"Parcel Porter was good too, we would have a flatbed trolley and we would have to unload a wagon full of mail bags, each about half full of lumps."

"Lumps?" Several of the populace were chuckling happily.

"Parcels, but they were just lumps, lumps with corners. You stacked them lumps to the outside, all round the edge of the flatbed in one layer then a line down the centre, to pin in place the tops of the bags forming the outside ring, then another ring round the outside and so on, upwards."

"I know. The second layer interleaving the first. Like stretcher bond bricks in a wall."

"Exactly, Rita. If you were a good stacker you could pile them twenty feet high on a flatbed trolley. The inspector, he was like a foreman, used to go apeshit because they were too tall to go through the doors, he knew we did it just for bad; he was a nice old stick, used to react specially for us. Then we'd sling a few off again, to please him."

"What about commerce?"

"Like, Ben, I've worked in a Greengrocer's. And at Christmas I've sold Christmas trees at a market garden."

Half way through another anecdote about roping up a wagon with hitches, and consequently, if you weren't careful, accidentally smashing up what you were roping on, the end of lesson bell went and Mr Baques had to hurry to finish it and re-endorse his support for work experience.

"Take anything! You never know until you try!"

Nobody was stupid enough to have a go at Roger over the incident, but the boy himself was more careful what he said in Mr Baques' presence, from then on.

Chapter 10

July 1986

Rita

High Trefoille Church Hall hosted a ceilidh a couple of Saturday nights a month. The place was packed out, mainly with locals from the Five Villages, but there were usually a substantial number of incomers. A couple of local bands provided the bulk of the nights entertainment, but there was a red-haired singer too, Poppy liked her, she went for the seriously difficult stuff and gave a good account of herself in doing so.

The working girl knew Colin lived nearby and kept looking for him in the crowd. He was there and, when their eyes locked, he smiled and nodded to her, she smiled back.

If -- She resolutely forced her mind empty of If Onlys and resumed scintillating for the pleasure of her escorts, three businessmen from the city, regulars, who paid well for good service.

After getting home in the small hours and remembering to switch the alarm to silent, Rita crept exhausted into Junty's sleeping bag. Propitiously, it was empty.

It was still empty, except for her, when she woke up, in time to make herself brunch.

Junty arrived half way through her homework.

"There's stew. And steamed pudding for afters. It'll have to be evaporated milk though, there's no custard."

"It's all yours dearie, I caught up with Frank. He's only here Saturdays; he's based in Shields. We're going to give it a try. You can have the bag and the kitchen, don't forget to reset the alarm each morning." He paused: "This quest of yours, to find yourself?" Rita laid her pen down,

"Yes."

"You're looking for a tree in a wood. Just look around you. This dump has been a nice home for over a year, nearly two, because of you. I'm moving on to higher things, confident that I can succeed, because of you." He shook his head: "You're Rita Roundheels, Miss Smarty-Pants-Brain-1986 and all round Goody-Box. When you find your higher things, ring this number." He pressed a little card into her hand: "I'll come and pick up anything I want to keep. Bye dearie." He kissed her.

"Bye. Good luck."

"And you. Promise me something."

"What?"

"Pretty Please."

"Okay."

"Stay off the streets, stick to the clubs. One conviction's way enough, it's one too many."

"I'll try."

"Just do it, none of this try, get out dodge."

Rita waited until the car that she now realised had been waiting for him, had drawn away with her friend safely aboard,

"I'm happy for you Junty. But, mangled floppies! Just where do I go from here?"

Chapter 11

July 1986

Sebastian

The prospect of a week's Work Experience, in a textiles and clothing factory, filled Sebastian with dread, but by the time he got his turn to dip into the Work Experience Placements Barrel, all the goodies had gone, only apparent scrapings were left in the bottom. He made his protest to his Form Tutor,

"It's not right you know Miss, there should be good placements for everyone."

"Like there are good jobs for everyone?" Miss J'Enson asked innocently.

Seb then accepted the placement with, for him, poise,

"Well there should be!"

Being forced to rub shoulders with hard-bitten, factory-floor girls, who eyed him up like a tasty lunch,

"Fancy your chances pet?"

"Wait 'til we catch him alone in the Stock Room!"

And gracefully give way to elegant typists that glanced once at his scuffed shoes and looked straight through him from then on, merely increased his sense of resentment.

By Wednesday and the start of a two day introduction to Salesman Techniques, he was ready to revolt. It began quietly enough with an illustrated lecture on the firm's products and a basic outline of how to sell them to customers who would not be buying by the each, but by the lorry-load. The climax of the two days for the group of Trainee Salesmen and pupils on Work Experience was the chance to act out an improvised selling appointment with a client. The five youngsters were sat down in a waiting area and told they would be selling to a client in the next room. A pimply youth was called forward and sent in.

"Where's he gone?" asked Sebastian.

"He's gone to sell his products to the commercial buyer."

"That's not right! And this exercise is supposed to be real? We are to **go for it!**"

"Yes."

Sebastian grabbed his case and followed the other youth into the room. The protestations of the instructor were ignored.

Inside, the blonde, pimply youth was crouched in the centre of the room, struggling with the clasps on his case. Sebastian strode past him extending his hand towards the man sitting at the desk.

"Good afternoon, Mr Body. Sebastian Stripe, Toptofty Textiles. You are going to enjoy the next half hour." He laid his case down on the desk facing the seated figure, opened it with a flourish and a slight jerk to flare out the cloth samples and seductively drape them over the edge of the case.

"This is our new series of fabrics, which is divided into four colour ranges, Pre-Teen, Young Miss -- so no section of society will feel neglected. Now the quality is -- Just feel these, beautiful aren't they -- which means that all modern machinery can handle the bales, no need to retool -- Now Sir, any questions before we settle down to discuss orders and quantity discounts?"

At the debriefing later,

"Exactly why did you barge in on your competitor?"

"He was in selling to the buyer, we're not going to sell anything to somebody who has a warehouse already stuffed with stock that isn't shifting. I had to get in first to prevent the buyer from making a serious mistake."

* * *

The following Monday Sebastian came home from school, to find his Dad holding an envelope sporting the Toptofty Logo.

"Your Mum doesn't know it's here, I suggested she visit Maud's and she's gone. Just in case it's a writ."

"I did nothing wrong. It was a stupid setup, it was supposed to be real, but it was a setup."

Seb Senior did not reply, just handed the letter over with a blank look.

Nodding and with a glum face, Sebastian opened the envelope with shaking hands and great difficulty and slid the letter out. The words jumped about on the page, but five of them stood out, as if in bold type:

attend for a job interview

he handed the letter over to his Dad,

"I can't hold it steady enough to read it, but I don't think it's a writ."

Chapter 12

October 1986

Colin

Colin decamped from the train and walked up the hill to school, planning his evening. Even if he got home quickly, he'd have to really shake it to get the flock down off the fell before dark. After juggling the options, he decided he'd try for it anyway, it would ease the weekend jobs considerably; there was plenty time in his weekend for the task, but it was fragmented. He grounded his school-bag and leaned against the ancient, grime-blackened stone wall of the cycle shed, to wait for Seb and Roger.

Unusually it was Roger who arrived first.

"What happened?" Colin asked him: "Not been home?"

"Got the wrong bus. Bloody sure it said 32, but it went the short way, 32A route, straight here. It's stupid, since they changed the routes you, like, never know where you're going."

"Well as least you're not late."

"You know bloody fine I wanted to be late, it's Wednesday. Assembly! I've not been to assembly for two years."

Colin shook his head, how on Earth had he stayed friends with such a tearaway?

"It's all right for you, Goody-Two-Shoes," Roger continued his rant: "But I've got, like, a reputation to keep up."

"You're as bad as Seb, he's busting a gut trying to manufacture one. Why bother? Just be yourself, I'm sure there must be a decent bloke in there, somewhere." He nodded significantly at the other's body: "The friend I used to have."

"I'm your friend because I put up with the smell, nobody else would. Except, like, Seb who smells even worse."

"My bag only fell in the sty once, as you well know. You're my friend because I'm useful to you. And, Seb hasn't smelt since the second year, since we told him. Here he is. Grinning. That date he was supposed to be fixed up with last night must have gone okay."

The senior boys leant against the cycle sheds, waiting morosely for school to start, while Seb boasted of his successful seduction.

"She was a right little scrubber, real teaser, but I showed her, knocked her good, knocked her up most probably."

The young-farmer, at the other end of the lounging line, had registered the errors of ignorance and wasn't buying.

"Sounds to me more like fantasy."

"Not everybody has their own private herd of cows to shag, whenever they want."

Colin made no reply, everyone knew he had sold his cows, although he still had lots of sheep, which, had he been so inclined, would have been much easier targets. Besides the pigs, some fowl and assorted small stock, his only other possessions were massive debts. The retort had as much grasp on reality as the seduction.

"I might go looking for her next Saturday, cut myself another slice."

"Like, in your dreams." The lad with the unfashionable Teddy boy hair cut and long bushy sideburns, leaning between the other two, took a last draw on his fag, then flung the glowing stub at a passing youngster, where it bounced off her plaits and lodged in her bag. Angrily, she retrieved it and threw it away, but walked on without comment.

"Cut that out, Roger," murmured the farmer.

"Like, what do you care!" replied the bully with a snarl.

"She wasn't doing anything."

"She's, like, a little stuck up professional virgin."

"Said no, did she?"

"Divot off Cadaver!" The other just ignored the reply and the usual cruel pun on his name, because a thin lad had coasted into the yard, half dismounted from his bike. There'd be trouble, there was usually trouble and Roger was obviously in one of his moods.

"Just leave him, he's harmless," said the farmer, trying to soothe.

"He's a geek. When he starts work he'll, like, be a scab." Although months on from that strike and all its hidden agendas, it was still possibly the worst insult he could hurl. They all saw the look of contemptuous fear in the thin boy's eyes, when he saw the group. He dismounted completely and walked past, the righteous disdain as tangible as a blow. Roger stepped forward, grabbed the saddle of the bike and with a vicious jerk rotated it almost half a turn, then stood back with folded arms. The cyclist's eyes were filling with tears, but he managed to walk away before they compounded his misery. Further into the yard he began unsuccessfully to attempt to re-turn the saddle.

"You didn't have to do that."

"Like, what do you care, he's a stuck up little prick and I hate him."

"He's done nothing to you."

"Thinks he's so superior, well, he isn't."

"He'll have to walk home, pushing it. Mind it's English last lesson, if Boris gets him in his stock cupboard again, he'll have to walk anyway." The would-be seducer roared with laughter at his own joke. "He won't be able to sit down."

"Everything's a sex related canard with you. You're sick." The farmer, walked away towards the vandalised bike, ignoring the insults hurled from behind him. "Is it okay?"

"Piss off."

"If you just walked past, didn't look, ignored him, he'd leave you alone."

"No he wouldn't."

"He thinks you think you're better than he is, if you ignored him, he'd stop. Do you want a hand?"

"Just piss off."

Colin walked on with a shrug; there was a far more interesting conversational target nearby.

"Hi, Rita, did you enjoy the ceilidh on Saturday?"

"It was business. But Poppy enjoyed it."

Colin knew full well Rita had been working; she only dressed like a tart when she was being one. Strangely, his feelings for her were only heightened by the absolute knowledge that she fucked for money, the urge to save her, protect her and shield her from further harm, was very strong.

"That redhead's got bottle. The Canadian girl. She tries difficult songs."

"Yes, she's often there. I'll let you know the next time she's on, if you like."

"Yes. Thank you Colin." The smile was friendly and all the way up to the eyes. "That would be nice. Please do." He sauntered off back the way he had come; the morose pall had lifted considerably.

"You know what she is, don't you!" The statement oozing spite had come from the head still bent over the twisted saddle.

"Yes, Ben, I do, but more to the point, so does she. People like that are scarce." The bell rang and he headed off into school, muttering: "There's some folks, you just can't do anything for, if you try, you end up regretting it."

After school, by sprinting to catch the early train, the farmer won himself a vital extra hour of daylight.

When Colin arrived at Trefoille-Halt, Sergeant Beaks was talking to the country station porter. The railwayman's duties also included occasional railway handyman and occasional stationmaster. The policeman looked the other way until the schoolboy had crossed over the road into the field, closed the gate behind him, started up his Landrover pickup and driven it safely away out of sight, up the farm track.

Colin dropped his books off and loaded up the pickup with hay for the stock.

“Come on you two, work to do.” The border collies leapt into the back of the Landrover. Together they headed out to round up the flock and move them down off the moor into a lowland field.

Even though none of the sheep had found a way through the ancient fence-topped walling that sliced across the county, marking the boundary between safe moor land and treacherous bog, it was getting dark by the time they were safely transferred.

With a smug feeling of satisfaction at having created some space in his crowded life, Colin headed homewards sedately and, for a short distance, illegally, along the quiet country road.

“What the--?” A vehicle ahead of him, swerved erratically, braking unpredictably.

Chapter 13

October 1986

Poppy

Poppy climbed out of Jingle's battered and asthmatic little car and the pair of them set off into The Swan pub for a sandwich before heading back to Novochester and their usual beat. Once inside, however, a group of punters with bulging wallets descended on the girls. Jingle was quickly spirited away by an occasional client.

"You go. I'll make my own way back. On the train."

The two young business executives, boys in men's bodies that she was left with offered Poppy drinks.

"Just orange please."

"They do a lovely orange and pineapple here, can I get you one?" Asked the nice boy.

"Yes please."

Half way down the second drink Poppy began to feel hot, then somehow the drink was finished and she was outside being helped into a car.

"No." Her legs felt strange. "I don't want to get--" The squab of the rear seat smacked her gently in the face, then she felt her unresponsive legs being pushed in. The door closed. The girl clawed herself upright, but by then they were out of the car park and making time along the road out of the village. The boys were arguing.

"Just give her her fee. It's only twenty-five."

"I've never paid for it yet and I never will," replied the pushy one, with an edge to his voice.

"She'll do anything for twenty-five and there'll be no hassle afterwards."

"She'll do anything for free, because you'll be holding her down." Poppy had heard enough and thought it prudent to decamp.

The door refused to open, even though the button was up. She wound the window down. The inrush of cold air alerted the others to her actions immediately. They began to shout at her and swerve the car about.

"Grab her!"

"I can't! I can't get to her!"

"I'll stop. You grab her!"

Despite being thrown about,

and the frantic attempts to grapple with her from the front seat,

she doggedly hauled herself up,

leaned out and opened the door from the outside.

It swung wide.

She was dragged with it,

and launched into the night.

Chapter 14

October 1986

Colin

Someone seemed to be leaning out of a nearside window. The car braked hard and stopped, as a door opened and a limp rag doll catapulted out onto the wide grass verge and rolled to a stop in a ravel of arms and legs. Another passenger jumped out, looked back at the approaching pickup, shut the rear door, jumped back aboard and the car left in a hurry of squealing, smoking tyres.

"Oh no!" Colin had already identified the bundle of familiar risqué clothes, making ineffectual efforts to stand up, that had been discarded on the muddy verge. He pulled over anxiously, dived out and ran round to her. Crouching down, he gathered her up to a sitting position in his arms: "Rita are you hurt? Do you want to go to hospital?"

"Poppy! Not Rita, dressed like this. No." The words were strong but slurred. "Not hurt. Suckered." She tried to look at him, but her eyes were unfocussed: "Not Hospital -- Home." Colin heaved her into his little truck, belted her into the seat and headed for home. She sat blinking at the passing signposts glaring their message in the headlights and occasionally turned to blink at him.

"Are you sure you're okay?"

"Will be. Orange juice. I mean pineapple. Very sweet. Must have been Vodka. Not medic. Just need time." Colin turned into his farm gate and parked at the back door.

"I need to feed the dogs, will you be okay?"

"What dogs? Haven't got any dogs."

"My dogs."

"Oh. Yes, feed dogs," said the swaying face.

When he returned to care for his girl, he took a flannel with him and cleansed her face and hands, before attempting to move her into the light.

"I can walk."

"I've never had a better chance of grabbing hold of you and I'm making the most of it."

Her deep throaty chuckle was most reassuring and she helped with an arm round his neck, whilst maintaining a seated position in his arms. "There's towels and stuff in the bathroom, in here, have a shower. I'll look out some of my sister's gear for you."

The heavy double thud from the downstairs bathroom had him returning at the run. He burst in before he thought it through.

Rita lay in a wriggling crumpled heap on the floor. That she was most probably unhurt became apparent because her hands were still trying to peel her knickers from her legs, while her bare bottom was pumping jerkily at him. Her top half was hidden under the washbasin.

"Sorry," came a muffled voice: "Wrong. Can't stand properly. Can you get knickers? Done the rest."

Animal urges flooded his groin; he peeled the wispy garment away and was treated to a pulse hammering, full reveal, as Rita squirmed about, but failed to rise.

Desperate not to grope, he gingerly reached in for her arms,

"Sit up, steady now," he said and hauled her out. This was immeasurably worse, the loveliest girl he knew was sitting on his Dad's bathroom floor, in a spread-legged sprawl and, smears of mud and hair adornments apart, she was newborn-baby naked.

October 1986: Colin

His body screamed with passion.

"Please wash me," she said, as her head wobbled unsteadily towards him. She closed her eyes and reopened them focusing upon him with difficulty. "Can't see properly."

Her matter of fact response to the situation allowed him to regain some control and concentrating on preparing the shower, helped force the reaction to back down.

Showering her down, while she knelt unsteadily on all fours in the bath, however, proved too much. When her nipples shot out to attack his soapy hands as they passed, his erection rearranged his underwear like a rampaging bull.

"Sorry," she giggled: "They do it. Not me."

"It's okay." He lied, rinsing her off. "Can you dry yourself, while I get you some clothes, nightie and stuff?"

"Try."

The clothes in his sister's wardrobe provided several close size matches and he sat her down, dressed decently in nightie and dressing gown, to a supper of chops, potatoes and vegetables.

"Sorry," she said between mouthfuls. "Don't drink often. Didn't drink tonight. They spiked my drink. Bundled me in the back. Couldn't open the door."

"Child locks?"

"Yes. Wound window down. Opened the door. They slowed, I went AWOL." She put her knife and fork down: "Sorry. Crashing out."

"Of course, I'll just lock up, there's some stock to see to and the dogs and that." When he returned the empty dishes were neatly stacked on the table, with his half finished meal, as he had left it. He found Rita lying face down on his mother's side of the only bed he bothered to keep made up, she'd pulled the covers back and almost managed to get in. He slid her legs and feet in and covered her. Then regretfully returned to clear up and do his homework. A couple of hours later, when he joined her, she hadn't moved.

Colin woke up before the alarm as he always did and slid out of bed before he gave in to the temptation that he'd successfully resisted all night. He showered and dressed and carried some more clothes through to his guest.

"Come on sleepy head, time to rustle. If you're well enough to go that is."

"I think so." She sat up: "Didn't have that much. But on an empty stomach --"

"How many eggs? Bacon? Cereal?"

"One egg, toast and coffee please. I know you farm boys eat for two. Last night's dinner would have fed a small country. This working girl doesn't."

"Last night's dinner was intended for two nights, but used for a much better purpose and Poppy's clothes are in the wash, please get up, Rita," he said formally and turned away to see to breakfast.

When she joined him for the meal, there was a lot of thigh on show, all of it scrumptious.

"Where is everybody?"

"There's only me, Mum left months ago, took Jane with her, left me with Dad. He died soon after, so I had to run the farm myself, but I'd been doing that for years anyway. Come on eat up, or we'll be late, you can copy my homework if you want."

"No. Thanks for the offer, but it's okay. I planned to do most of it at lunchtime anyway. I'll do the Physics on the train."

"And still come top of the Year."

Rita shrugged: "I'm lucky. No effort. For some folk, I think it is hard work."

"I'm glad I kept Jane's stuff, most of it's a good fit." Rita looked down at the school uniform she was wearing,

"She liked her skirts short mind!"

"You look good in it." She dropped him a curtsy.

"Thank you. You're nice."

"I'll have to do something about that, no street cred in nice." Colin was eying up two rolls of brisket: "Poppy's stuff's not ready, come back tonight?"

"Okay." He plucked both rolls up and plonked them into a slow cooker, along with a selection of vegetables and stock. After switching it on, he checked the setting and the lights,

"Let's go."

When he got in the Landrover.

"You're not old enough."

"Most of it's cross-country, the Authorities pretend they don't know about the bit that isn't. I don't push it; they ignore the fuzzy edges."

"Oh, right." Rita climbed in beside him, belted herself in and held on tightly as the 4x4 lurched down the track. She studied the fencing and walling as they passed. "Why do some walls have fences on top of them?"

"Sheep. A two-metre stone-wall is merely a handy way of getting from one field to another for a black-faced hill sheep. They just run up it, straight over the top and down the other side, the wire stops that."

"But a one metre wire fence keeps them in?"

"Sort of, I think it's because they can see through it, so they try to find a hole that they can wriggle through, they don't seem to realize they can jump it, so it keeps them in, mostly. Until they find a hole. Sheep are like octopus; they can get through a hole smaller than their own head. Well it seems that way sometimes!"

Inside school she thanked him and the pair spent the day treating each other completely normally, usually in the same room and rarely more than two or three metres apart, as if nothing had happened.

At the end of school, he found her discussing a gymnastics competition, with her friends outside the girl's gym and just quietly waited to one side. She joined him without making any attempt to hide the fact.

"Do you need to collect anything, bring it home with you?"

"Home? I agreed to come back tonight, did you have more in mind."

"Yes, quite a lot more. I'd need time to explain everything." There was a long pause; several of Rita's friends were unashamedly rubbernecking.

"What's at the squat's not mine. There's a bag in the left luggage. At the station. I'll need it if I'm staying, we could pick that up."

"Okay."

She turned back to her friends,

"Best put all my training arrangements for the competition on hold. For now. I'll let you know as soon as."

"Okay."

At home, Rita saw to the evening meal and did some housework, while Colin tended his stock and repaired a gate. The youngsters sat together at the table, doing their homework.

"All finished?" he asked.

"Think so. Yes."

"Come on then, we'll make up a bed for you."

"We slept together last night -- I haven't slept alone for four years. Apart from the odd night." The pair stood looking at each other. "Colin, close to a thousand men have had what my body has to offer. And a lot of women. Most of it anyway. And I didn't like some of them. I wouldn't mind one I liked having all of it. I'd quite like it."

"A thousand men have had Poppy, that's not what I want. I want Rita, not just Poppy's body and not to share. I'd like you to live here, work on the farm, not go back to your old job."

"Weeks trial?"

"A year. That way, you can see it all, the farmer's year."

"Work on the farm. Sleep in your bed. Look after your house. In effect be your wife. For a year?"

"Something like that -- very like that -- exactly that." She stuck her hand out,

"Farmer Colin. You have a deal. I need to make a telephone call." she checked her watch: "No. Tomorrow will do." She released his hand and snuggled into him. "Have you done it before?"

"Sort of, Jane and I, we had a giggly-sexy holiday with some cousins a few years back. We slept in the tree house; nobody came to check who was sleeping where. And when we pulled up the rope ladder, they couldn't anyway. Jane slept with Jack the whole week and, after the first night, when Faye and Tuesday realised their big brother was occupied with his own private cuddly toy, they took me to bed with them. It was nice and I loved it. I was probably too young to give them a really good time, but they were very nice about it." He looked at her apologetically. "They gave **me** a really good time."

"Good. Take me to bed. Let's see if we can have a giggly-sexy really good time."

"Wow! Thank you, that was lovely, did you--"

"Yes I did. That was what all the screaming was about. So thank you too Farmer Colin. Your cousins probably had a better time of it than you suspect. My guess."

"Oh, I'd like to think so."

"I know so. Anytime you want an encore. Five minutes time. Five hours. Just climb aboard. I want a lot more of that. Often." There was a silence. "What is it? -- Just say it darling."

"Tuesday used to like it lying face down."

Rita spun into position.

"Like this? Doggy style?"

"Yes -- I suppose so."

"Come on then nice doggy. Please your mistress."

Colin and Rita waited behind after Assembly the following morning to speak to their Form Tutor.

"Miss J'Enson, I've moved."

"Oh. Right, I'll need some details."

"I've written them all down for you."

"Great that's exactly what I nee -- Vertlea Farm, High Trefoille, that's -- it's --"

"Colin's place, Yes Miss. I've moved in with him."

"Oh, has your Mum come back, or Jane?"

"No Miss. There's just the two of us."

"Oh. Right. Okay."

"When I'm not **here**, I'll be working full time on the farm."

Miss J'Enson looked up sharply. Rita met her eyeball to eyeball, unflinching.

"Message received and understood," replied the teacher.

After a meeting with the Deputy-Head Pastoral, Mr Baques was able to downgrade the pair's status in the Danger Register from Red for Rita and Amber for Colin, to Green for both of them.

Chapter 15

November 1986

Rita

It was a week later when Sergeant Beaks called in,

"I've virtually been sent by the Social, they seemed reluctant to come any nearer than High Trefoille, to check up on you. Well specifically you Miss."

"I'm sixteen too."

"That's what I needed to hear Miss. Can you prove it please?" Colin produced her passport from a dresser drawer and handed it over. "That's fine. Do your parents know where you are?"

"No. You might tell me where they are. If you can find them. Mum ran off after a cute butt. Again. But this time without me. That was four years ago. John flitted while I was away. At guide camp, two years ago. When I got home I had to break in. To get my clothes. He'd provided for me, a bit anyway. Which was kind of him. He wasn't my real father, but the best Dad I'd ever had. I've not heard from them since. We were just about to have coffee?" She held up a mug to emphasize the invitation.

Sergeant Beaks grimaced, waving at the rain thrashing across the Fells,

November 1986: Rita

"It's a foul day out and the Social Workers are waiting and The Village shut as soon as they saw who it was. They really need me back quick, before they die of boredom, trapped in their car." He grinned broadly: "So yes please Miss and while I'm here there's something else, something nice."

Intrigued, the young couple sat the policeman down, gave him his coffee and waited expectantly. "My spies in the big city tell me that you write stories, I mean **quality** stories."

Colin enlightened her,

"He's Boris' brother, sorry, I mean Mr. Beaks."

The burly Copper gave no reaction, he just sat looking steadily at Rita; she was non-committal,

"Things have been said."

"Every Christmas we do a pantomime in the Church hall. The kids from the Five Villages. Every year it gets harder to find something new, last year we had to hire a professional script, which cost a fortune and decimated the money we raised for charity." Rita looked up at her boy, who, without a word, retrieved a notepad and pencil from the dresser and put them down in front of her.

"Which ones have you done recently?" she asked, pencil poised. While Rita jotted notes, the policeman reeled off a list, finishing with,

" -- we had to do Aladdin and Jack and the Beanstalk twice because of the cost of the costumes and the set."

"Little Miss Muffet?"

"No. Is that a Pantomime?"

"I can make it into one. Which is what you want. Isn't it?"

"Well, yes."

"It needs neither set, nor costumes, except the obvious one of course. It's got a vulnerable heroine. A simple setting. All it needs is a hero. To show his true colours when tested. It's already got a surprise hero's helper. And of course we need oppressed villagers. And a truly hiss-able villain."

"Spiders are pretty hiss-able for most people, personally I like 'em mind, you know where you are with spiders."

"The spider's not the villain. She's the helper. I've got a real villain in mind. Currently freezing in a car in the Village. We're talking ruthless ambition, theft and betrayal." She began to sketch the outline of a plot, scene by scene in a list down the paper. "Treachery and possibly murder. Just what young kids love." A couple of entries were squeezed in between existing ones as afterthoughts. "And Good triumphant eventually, of course." The list was complicated even further by arrows re-arranging some entries. She passed the pad over: "What d'y'think?"

"I think Boris has you sussed, he said you'd be a writer eventually. When do you think you'll have something for the Pantomime Sub-Committee?"

"A week on Friday. Mebees."

* * *

Back at school, their Art teacher was most helpful about the pantomime project,

"Anything you need, if we've got it you can borrow it."

"The camouflaged muslin sheet. Have you any books that show examples of camouflage colour schemes?"

"Why don't you ask Shelley to do it for you?"

"We couldn't afford her! Her work sells in town for over two grand!"

"Which is about one thousandth of its true value! Your pantomime is for charity, she'd do it for free. Look, William's next door, ask him."

Rita walked through to the other Art room to find the Sixth Former who had fallen in love with child-like Shelley and was now making a successful career for the pair of them as The Artist's business partner,

"William I need a sheet of muslin camouflaged for a kid's pantomime." She outlined the scene and explained what she wanted. "So I was wondering if Shelley would do it?"

"Here she comes now, we'll have to grab her quick before The Artist starts work and switches the World off."

Shelley came into the room and lit up when she saw her boy,

"My hands are happy," she said.

"Hello darling, can I speak to the artist?"

"Yes."

William outlined Rita's requirements,

"Can you do it?"

"What colour is the background?"

Rita never ceased to be amazed at how different The Artist's deep, manly-voice was to that of the schoolgirl, she even looked different.

"Shades of grey. A symbolic castle wall, sinister."

"You will need it to be unhappiness greys and sinister greens. Jagged flashes of angry red. I'll hide the violet anchor in a fold. Have you got the muslin?"

"It's downstairs."

"I need it now! I need to run it--"

"Go and get it now, Rita, she'll have mixed the paint by the time you get back."

Just before end of school a messenger arrived with a note. Rita's teacher read it,

"Is anyone expecting a note from Shelley? About a commission."

Rita put her hand up,

"Me, Miss."

Her teacher gave her the note,

"Don't throw that note away, Rita, it's probably worth a hundred pounds to a collector, even better, keep it with the work, it's priceless provenance."

The note was in the Artist's familiar script.

Please come to check your commission,

Michelle.

1986.

William was waiting for her in the art-room; Shelley was busy at a canvas in the adjoining room.

"Well? What do you think?"

Rita looked for her muslin,

"Where is it?"

William began to smile,

“Exactly.”

A second look around her still failed to reveal the whereabouts of the muslin.

“I can’t see it.”

William raised his arms, fingers flared, making like a letter Y, the smile had become a broad grin,

“It’s hanging on the wall behind me,” he said through his chuckles.

* * *

When the Sub-Committee read the first outline draft of the script, they found themselves energetically hissing at the machinations of the villains, whilst laughing out loud at the antics of the well-meaning, but bumbling vicar, whose unintentional cross-dressing was childishly funny up front, and on the double-entendre level, seriously funny for adults.

--

Scene: Empty stage, backdrop of a low hedge. Corner of stone church in view left. Small rock right. Enter Vicar and Curate stage right, carrying a bucket and a dish–washing mop.

VICAR: We need to wash that window.

(*Points up out of sight. Curate looks pointedly at the mop in his hand. He mimes reaching up. The handle is obviously too short.*)

CURATE: Can’t reach it.

VICAR: Never mind I’ll throw the water up.

CURATE: Get wet when it comes down.

VICAR: Hmm. (*Looks around for people.*) I’ll take my habit off then, there’s nobody here. You stand well back.

(*Takes habit off facing front. Reveals one piece long-john underwear. When laughter stops he turns and drapes habit over rock. Revealing ‘Made in China’ written across his bottom.*)

CURATE: Standing well back.

VICAR: Okay.

(*Picks up bucket and throws contents high stage left. Engulfed by huge dump of blue and white polystyrene granules from above. Vicar collapses under it.*)

I'm soaked!

(*Curate rushes over to help. Unseen by audience vicar douses his front in shaving cream. Spider enters stage right. Fingers habit.*)

SPIDER: A nishe coat for the poor shildren of the parish. I'll sheize it for them, thish moment.

(*Takes habit and departs right. Vicar stands up covered in foam and polystyrene.*)

CURATE: Soaked. Have to go straight home. Get your Habit -- It's not here.

VICAR: Find it! You've got to find me something! Get me something quick.

(*Curate runs off stage right. Vicar cleans off some of the debris. Curate returns carrying clothes.*)

CURATE: These are all could find. They're off Miss Muffet's washing line.

(*Holds up short dancing skirt and sequined top.*)

VICAR: I can't wear that.

CURATE: *(Bundling him into the clothes.)* It's that or nothing. Hurry people are coming.

(*Curate and Vicar moonwalk on the spot centre stage. Church disappears stage left. Rock moves towards stage left. They crouch down behind rock as villagers walk past on the other side of the hedge. Villagers look at the hiding pair but say nothing. Repeated twice with ever-smaller rocks. Vicarage door appears stage right.*)

VICAR: We're home. Just the main road.

CURATE: Full of people.

VICAR: I'll put my bucket on my head. Nobody will know it's me.

(*Puts bucket on head. Strides across to the door. Miss Muffet opens it and greets him.*)

MISS MUFFET: Hello Vicar, I've put your kettle on they said you were coming.

VICAR: (*From inside bucket.*) Who said?

MISS MUFFET: Everybody. I've got an outfit just like that one. I got mine at Top Shop, where did you get yours?

--

Only Mrs. Guggenheim, who regularly identified unflattering references to herself in the annual production and thus never attended, took any exception to the script. This outbreak of normality, removed any lingering doubts anyone else may have had. 'Little Miss Muffet, adapted by Poppy', as the next Pantomime, went through, on the nod.

Sergeant Beaks brought her the news the following day,

"It's a go. When do you think you can have it finished, rough cut?"

"When do you need it by?"

"October week? But that's only three weeks or so."

"You said it could be quite short. With it being mostly children performing it. I could have an hour. Hour and a bit, ready by then. We need to leave space to comment on news items anyway. Last minute jokes."

Sergeant Beaks nodded, then broached the other subject,

"Where's, Colin?"

"Bollyfaith Moss. Some of Jill's sheep got through. He's helping her round them up."

"We've got a new young Inspector at the Station, want's all the records Computerised, put on a National Database."

"Oh! Well it was inevitable. I guess."

"I pulled your record as a first priority, brought it up to date and typed it in. I think it's just as important to have solid evidence of people going straight recorded, or even more important than the other."

"Oh. Thanks."

"How much does Colin know, if it's not a rude question?"

"It's not a rude question. The answer is everything."

The policeman visibly relaxed,

"That's great, that's -- that's fine. Any clients in the Five Villages that might be a problem?"

"Not to me. I'll sharp let you know if anyone is. One of the things that living on the streets taught me. You can't have too many friends. All my regulars were good friends. Most of the ones where once was once too many, don't know it."

The pantomime was well into rehearsal, when somebody belatedly thought about asking the vicar if he minded being lampooned in this way.

"I don't mind, but there is a problem, if it's the Five Villages doing the Pantomime, as usual."

"I knew things were going too smoothly." said Sergeant Beaks: "What is it?" He jerked upright: "You're not really a transvestite are you?"

"No."

"Thank goodness for that.

"But the Vicar at Low Trefoille is and he was deep in the closet. You've unintentionally outed him."

Chapter 16

November 1986

Sebastian

Having a job already in his pocket steadied Seb down considerably. He no longer felt obliged to create an image and only joined in the conversation around him when he had something to say. The change although marked by everyone, came too late for the girls of his acquaintance. They were either already cuddled up elsewhere, or unwilling to trust that the leopard's spots weren't still there, under the zebra's stripes.

Every so often a pair of girls would sidle up to the boys and address one of them.

"My mate wants to go out with you."

Colin would ask the messenger to thank her mate for the invite, but gently decline it.

"I'm courting, say sorry, but thanks anyway."

Roger might ask,

"Which one is she?" Or occasionally cut crudely straight to the chase: "Does she shag?" If the girl was pretty, or the answer 'Yes,' the date would be fixed up.

Sebastian was never asked.

Whenever he had quizzed Roger about his dates before, the hard lad had chopped him off. Now suddenly, and to his astonishment, Seb realised he no longer had a burning desire to know. He would find out soon enough when he let some of the factory girls catch up with him in the stock room. But that would be when he chose to let it happen. The possibility filled him with excitement and dread in equal proportions and frequently fuelled his nightly sexual fantasies.

Several subjects began putting on extra classes at night and lunchtime. Sebastian turned up to the first one, mainly through a sense of duty and was rewarded by a mind-blowing status change in his learning.

"For example, Sebastian, your last homework. Three questions on heat calculations. Every one wrong, yet the first one was worked in the book for you. All you had to do was copy it down. The other two you had to work out, but they were the same as the first one, with different figures. Did you look at the book?"

"No of course not."

"Why not?"

"I don't cheat."

Mr Baques heaved a deep sigh,

"Not another one who does their homework under exam conditions?"

"Yes, of course."

"Who in the hot place is spreading this heresy?"

Sebastian was amazed to learn that he was expected to use his book to help him in his Physics homework and it so shook him to his core that no arguing thought surfaced.

Mr Baques was resigned that he had to stress to the boy that not only was this true for Physics, but for all other subjects too.

Sebastian turned up to the rest of the courses, entirely through choice.

There was a change at home too. Whereas he would still get comprehensively bawled out occasionally, the beatings stopped.

Why is open to speculation, his improved delivery of good work certainly helped, but it is an historical fact that he now towered over his Mum, although in his own eyes he still cowered. Ironically if anything this only made the creaking relationship worse and drove him more and more to seek solace by talking to his Aunt when she called in with shopping. The furtive caresses he gave himself in bed later were always accompanied by more spectacular fireworks, on nights following her visits.

The Stripe family holiday consisted of days away that June because Seb was up to his scalp in GCEs and for the first time in his life, sitting examinations for which he was reasonably well prepared.

Whether the nephew would ever pluck up enough courage to do anything about his secret incestuous passion for his young aunt became merely academic the following year.

Chapter 17

December 1986 -- October 1988

Rita

For most people, that there was now a young couple at Vertlea Farm was most encouraging. The doctor's wife mentioned the matter in the Post Office.

"I hear young Colin's wife is making her presence felt in the community already."

"That's her over there," murmured the postmaster. "She seems very nice and she can write a wickedly funny pantomime scene."

The fact that they were very young and unmarried, was quickly forgotten by the general populace. Only the predictable professional moaners found anything amiss and were further confounded when they discovered that Colin and Rita were amused by their fury.

Johann Beaks collected Rita and took her to the first read through of the pantomime, with the actors who would be performing it.

"There's only one real casting problem. The spider," said the teacher who would be producing it. "You have her leaping out over the audience to her web, slung out above their heads and pursuing the villains through the audience and out of the back of the auditorium. I don't see how we could stage that, we have no-one who could jump like that."

"Erm -- I was hoping you'd say that. I really wrote the part for me. I'm a gymnast. I could do the jump. Off a trampette. And the rest of her part needs no talent. She says next to nothing. In my mind. I have her as a papier mâché model. Except for that scene. And the habit and the cup of course."

"What cup?"

"It's in the latest version, today's latest amendment, hot off 'n that. It's during Mr and Mrs Villain from Social Service's picnic. Next to the tuffet?"

"When they finalize their plans to abduct Miss Muffet?"

"Yes. He rests his cup on Spiders head. She moves it off. And her eyes flash red. Pulsing red."

"Ooh. The other problem is just before the jump. How do we get you onto the middle of an empty stage unobserved?"

"That's even easier. I just walk on. No-one will see me. Honest."

"No-one?"

"Not even the four characters struggling on the stage. I promise you. Heroic Jack will have to trust I'm there. And shout for me. Even though he won't be able to see me. The success, the timing of the whole scene, rests on his shout."

The cast read and walked through the latest version of Miss Muffet, who, orphaned as a result of eating curds and whey, became the target of an abduction by Social Services. Later, as part of their baby farming business, she was to be sold off to rich Americans for a million Curly-Whirlies.

An eight-year-old member of the chorus fell hopelessly for Rita and followed her about, like an extra leg, gazing up at her in adoration. In the middle of the penultimate scene, where the spider appears from nowhere, to rout the villains, the little girl addressed her idol,

"But Miss Roundheels, I can see you."

"It's okay chick. I'm not hiding yet. I'll hide on the dress rehearsal. Try not to look for me. Watch Heroic Jack protecting Miss Muffet. Then afterwards you can tell me if you could see me."

The dress rehearsal was notable for the dame forgetting the news item just inserted that day and the spider spilling the drink on her own head.

During the fight scene however, where hero, heroine and villains fought it out for control of Miss Muffet, everyone was given a foretaste of how the members of the audience were going to react to the real performance.

Heroic Jack and Miss Muffet were dressed in brightly coloured spangles and sequins and the villains in black with diamanté highlights.

Against a darkened backdrop of the sinister grey walls of County Hall, powerful spotlights tracked the fight from the rear of the stage, zigzagging completely from side to side. It was a kaleidoscope of flashing lights lurching drunkenly about, until it had worked its way to the centre front, next to the footlights.

While the villains grabbed Miss Muffet, despite Heroic Jack's best efforts to protect her, Rita strode out to centre stage and climbed onto her tuffet, supremely confident that she was unobserved.

Mr Villain wrested Miss Muffet from Jack.

"At last we have her!" He shouted in triumph. "You'll never get her back!" Jack, almost defeated, but still holding on to one hand, shouted despairingly,

"Spider! Spider! I need you now!"

Crash of drums.

Flash of light.

The sheet of camouflaged muslin,
Rita was holding before her
was plucked off-stage on strings.

Two new spots on Spider.

Immediately behind the others.

Towering over them.

Red eyes flashing.

Fangs extended.

The chorus screamed.

Jack and Miss Muffet gasped.

The villains forgot to run and Rita had to feint an attack before they turned and pelted off the stage.

She pursued them, leaping over the chorus, to her web, six rows back, dropped down behind the fleeing pair and ran out after them.

The final scene had the cast eating mince pies and being waited on by Mr and Mrs Villain, bound from ankles to throat in polythene pallet-wrap masquerading as spider web, all except their lower arms, mincing about, carrying trays.

Whilst wiping Mrs Villain's greasepaint off herself afterwards, Jill turned to Rita,

"I couldn't see you, you know, I was five feet away and I couldn't see you."

"It's amazing. I could see you clearly. But I've stood on both sides of the muslin. It's one way only. And your fight of course. Like the magician's misdirection. Everyone's looking somewhere else. At you. Not at me."

There was a gentle touch against Rita's thigh. She looked down into the adoring eyes.

"I couldn't see you. I thought you weren't there. I'm so glad you were there."

"I could see you. Looking worried. Don't worry. I'll always be there. It's my big scene."

Every night the Spider's appearance produced a scream of appreciation from the audience, followed closely by another when, as the house-lights went up, she leaped over the front rows to her web and pursued the ungodly out of the auditorium.

The problems were voiced at the next Parish Council meeting,

"Next year, how on Earth do we follow that?"

And from the Treasurer:

"Mr Chairman I've had an offer of a thousand pounds for the Muslin."

"You've not accepted it I hope," said Johann Beaks.

"Well no, not yet." said the treasurer, shaking his head. "I--"

But Mrs Guggenheim interrupted,

"Why ever not?" She snorted.

"Because it's a Shelley Bomey which may not be ours and she signed and dated it," he replied patiently. "Which makes it worth more than your house! Or it soon will be. Get ownership established, then if it's ours, offer it for sale at one of the big auction houses, or advertise it privately, you'll get much more for it, I promise you."

Rita started on her second pantomime shortly after New Year. Just as she was completing the first draft, a chance glimpse of the assertive behaviour of a schoolgirl towards her boyfriend, whilst they were waiting for the train, had her writing an erotic short story that evening. Over the next few months, further more varied items, pictures in magazines, off beat news items and the like triggered more and more and increasingly salacious output from Poppy.

* * *

The third Thursday in August, Results Day, Rita turned up at school alone.

"Can I have Colin's too, please, Miss J'Enson?"

"Thank goodness for that," said her Form Tutor: "When you turned up alone, muddy -- I thought you might be squatting again -- but obviously not."

"No Miss. Nothing like that. We're set up. Long term plans. But we're very busy. The mud's off the Four-Acre. I was ploughing before I came over."

"Ploughing?"

"Yes Miss. Good fun. And by the new Millennium my furrows might be straight. But I doubt it."

"I didn't know you ploughed in August."

"Hill Farm, Miss. It's usually done in September for Winter Wheat, but we are a month to six weeks different from lowland more southerly farms. The Gulf Stream doesn't reach our little bit of Heaven."

"Oh, okay. Here they are. Congratulations."

"Oh," said Rita, looking down her straight 'A's list and Colin's very similar set. "Oh. Thanks. Colin will be pleased. He wasn't sure about French and History. He said to say, 'Thank

You!' For the last five years. Can you pass our thanks on to everybody? We can't spare the time. For Colin to be away, I shouldn't be here even."

At the end of her year's trial, Rita wandered slowly down the stairs opening curtains on her way. Colin was waiting for her in the hall: "Do you know what day it is?"

"Yes." She replied.

"Happy anniversary," he said, produced a bouquet of flowers and a card from behind his back and gave them to her.

"I knew you'd remember. I didn't forget either."

Rita opened her card and read,

All my love from me.

X X

X

"Thank you," she said.

Colin's present was a video he had mentioned that he might buy and his card contained a very similar greeting and,

Can I extend the trial a year?

They laughed and kissed,

"Of course you can have an extension, but I had something much more permanent in mind. Rita Roundheels, will you marry me?"

"No darling, one day perhaps. But I'll only marry you when I can bring something to the marriage." She silenced his protests with a finger and followed it up with kisses. "I'll be your faithful, common law wife. For as long as you like. Bear children for you. Anything. But I won't marry you. Not until I know who I am. And what I can bring to your life."

Colin held her tightly in silence for a while, then sighed deeply through his nose,

"I liked the sound of bear children."

"Okay, I'll come off the pill. At the end of this month. We'll see what happens."

What happened was twins, James and Jane, just under a year later.

* * *

Colin pushed the books away in disgust,

"We're going to make a loss again this year. I don't know what to do."

"Can I do the books for a while? See how it goes."

"Feel free, nobody will be more pleased than me if you keep us out of the red."

It took a lot of scrimping and saving and not a little re-assignment of resources, but Rita bent the graph back into the black, only just and only for the year, but black.

The following year they did a little better and the year after that paid a small amount off their debt. In addition to the annual Christmas adaptation, she wrote a number of short stories 'by Poppy', but Poppy's real life experiences kept popping up and Rita had to take over and rewrite a cooler version. Sporadically, every few weeks a small cheque arrived, as a magazine editor found room for one she liked.

"Why don't you write a story about the other thing you know well?"

"Which is?"

"Having and raising twins."

'P is for Panic, the first eighteen months after hearing the words: "It's twins" --' was half written when the telephone rang late one afternoon and, to Colin's greeting, an unfamiliar girl's voice asked,

"Hello, I'm not sure I've got the right number, can I speak to Poppy please?"

"Depends what about." he replied.

"Three Little Pigs, adapted by Poppy?"

"And you would be?"

"My name is Rachael Rowberts, but you've probably not heard of me." Colin held out the receiver to his girl,

"Rachael Rowberts wants to talk to the Poppy who adapted Three Little Pigs."

"She's an Agent. A Literary Agent. And that was quick. I only sent it to that weekly rep. last week. She must know somebody in the company."

The telephone conversation was short and businesslike and concluded with an appointment for Rachael to call in at teatime the following Thursday.

Consequently Rita was caught abeam when the agent arrived not only two hours, **but** also two whole days early.

* * *

Rachael Rowberts was young and energetic, almost wearing a flag on a stick proclaiming that she was eager to get on and make her name in the World of Publishing.

Oh no! Thought Rita: She's exactly what I need, but there's no way that I'm what she wants.

Chapter 18

June 1987 -- June 1988

Sebastian

"Now that you are starting your working life, can I do a makeover on you? What was good enough for school will not be good enough for work. Let me do the makeover?"

Sebastian looked into his young Aunt's eyes and read the message,

"Of course."

"It will need a lot from you."

"I had guessed that much."

"You've got your personal freshness sorted for mornings, but our family perspire a lot, so you need deodorant protection to last until you can get home and shower."

"I don't use deodorant."

"You do from now on."

"Oh -- Okay."

"Your suits must have at least two pairs of trousers. A jacket will last for several weeks, but trousers only one week between washes."

"Washes?"

"Yes, so buy washable ones."

"Oh."

"When you come home, take off your work suit and hang it up, that way it will last the week."

"Huh--"

"And none of that arguing young man. I'm not doing this makeover of you for you; it's entirely for me, because I am sick of having my favourite nephew appearing to be such a jerk. It upsets me. I know you will get nothing out of it, but **I** will."

Sebastian took a deep breath to protest and in doing so gave himself time to analyse his Aunt's words and sift the true meaning from the irony.

"I'm sorry -- I'm really sorry. Go on, no arguments, I'm listening and taking note."

"Part of the makeover is not to argue without thought. Think first and then if you still want to argue, think it through again and change your mind."

There was a long silence, slowly Seb relaxed,

"Okay."

"Now shirts, your tie will last a week, if you don't drop dinner down it, but your shirt will barely make it through one day. So you need several, about ten should --"

"-- shoes, people look at your shoes and make instant snap decisions. Often they don't realize they are doing it, but --"

Maud worked steadily through her makeover of Sebastian; presently realisation dawned on her nephew,

"What you're really saying is my former self wasn't good enough for school either."

"Occasionally, but that's all in the past. We are looking to the future. Will you do as I have said?"

"Yes, new job, new me."

Toptofty Textiles was a respected company in their field, manufacturing both cloth and clothes, at the quality end of the Rag Trade. On leaving school, Sebastian took up the proffered job as Trainee Sales Manager.

The important-sounding euphemism for gofer, was quickly turned into fact, when his bosses confirmed that the brass-necked, nudge-nudge, wink-wink, occasionally economical with the truth Old Boy, persona, was not a front. The World of Selling was one where Sebastian felt completely at home. Junior replaced Trainee and equally rapidly, became Assistant.

Lady Luck stepped in and jovially twisted the knife a couple of times.

The Sales Manager of Toptofty Textiles retired, and, when he was passed over in favour of a genuinely talented subordinate, the Buggins's-Turn choice, Deputy Manager replacement, left in a fit of pique. Within two years angina removed the sitting tenant on the Board and, yet again, everyone moved up one place, bouncing Sebastian into the job of Sales Manager.

Toptofty's Works' Annual Holiday coincided with Maud's Works' Holiday, but not with that of the rest of the Stripe family. The clash hadn't been a problem when Seb started work, both events were over, but the following year it was a source of tension. The topic came up in conversation one night, when Aunt Maud had called in with shopping for her sister. Against the wishes of both principals and Sebastian Senior, an arrangement that Seb should stay with his Aunt for the fortnight and accompany her on holiday for the following two weeks, was railroaded through by Mrs Stripe.

"I don't see why I can't just stay at home."

"Don't argue!"

"Colin's been running his farm alone for years--"

"As I understand it, he's far from alone. And it's exactly that sort of thing I'm not having in my house! You'll do as you're told and like it."

"And wha--"

"Don't you start! You have a duty to your kin Maud, the matter is decided."

Sebastian Senior dropped his son's case off at his sister-in-law's house on the Monday morning and his son at Toptofty.

"Now don't forget to go to the right house tonight. And go straight there from work. You don't want Maud getting worried about you."

"Yes Dad. I still--"

“Nor do I son. Just make the best of it for now. Perhaps when you’re older, we’ll think about it for next year.”

It was that Monday that the Deputy Manager resigned and walked out. Totally unsuspecting, Sebastian was called in to the Managing Director’s Office, where he was sat down and taken through a résumé of his progress.

“So, Sebastian, you are making good progress, do you plan to stay with us?”

“Yes I’ve been discussing some ideas with my line manager, we might have some plans to put to The Board soon. When they’re ready.”

“So I understand. You’ve been on two management courses, is that where you see yourself going?”

“Yes. Eventually.”

“How about now, today, this minute?”

“Pardon.”

“You’re Line Manager has resigned and left the company. I need a Deputy Manager now! The job is yours, on six months trial, if you want it.”

Sebastian paused, took a deep breath and said,

“Yes please.”

The rest of the day passed with Sebastian being swept along by the storm.

Moving offices, consulting files, speaking with clients, presently he didn’t know which way was West and began to worry and regret his hasty acceptance. Fortunately his new secretary, a middle aged pearl, had mentored inexperienced but potentially good managers before and guided him and steadied him throughout it all.

“May I go now Mr. Stripe? Just it’s half past six and--”

“What! I’m late! I’m late! Yes Mrs Brycee, go now, I’m late.”

“Can I drop you, I go through Ryker, to Vallumend.”

“St Paul’s Harbour?”

“I go right past the gate.”

Maud was waiting and opened the door for him as he reached it,

“Did you forget and go home? It doesn’t matter, as long as you’re all right.”

"No. No it wasn't that at all." To his horror, Sebastian burst into tears.

Maud hurriedly pushed the door shut and holding him, took him through into the living room and drew him down with her onto the sofa. She stroked his hair,

"Let it go, get it all out."

He exploded into huge racking sobs, the story gushing out of him.

The promotion thrust upon him, dangerous and frightening. She snuggled him against her voluptuous breasts, as always, braless inside the thin housecoat.

"It's what I wanted." He tried to clean his eyes and merely brushed the housecoat aside, releasing a soft compliant globe.

"But I'm too young, I'll mess it up and lose the chance." Maud nestled him against her, caressing his face with hers.

"The chance has come too soon. I'm not ready for it." When his further, fumbled, flicking away of tears, which were not designed to release the second breast, understandably failed to do so, she did it for him.

"Two years. Then I would have been ready, even possibly next year!"

The tirade slowed and stopped, at last he was aware that he was squeezing one voluptuous naked breast and all but suckling the other. He lifted off electrified.

"I'm sorry, I didn't mean it." Only Maud's strong wiry arms held him in place.

"I know, it's all right, I don't mind. Seb I don't mind. I think it's what you need." She assertively pulled his hand back to her breast and put his face to the other one. "Suck me. Suck hard, nibble gently. That's it, that's right. Your bosses know you're too young, they haven't set you up. No keep sucking, just listen. They don't expect you to perform miracles. But they will expect you to learn from your mistakes. Handle situations as you know your old boss would have done, but put your own style on it. If there are places where you think he was doing it wrongly, check, say you plan to do it differently, they may possibly be why he was passed over." Slowly Maud analysed the situation and cut it down to a manageable sized problem. Sebastian's erection was thrust hard into his aunt's thigh. He was going to move it away, but he realised there was little point, she must have been aware of it for some time. By now they were sprawled across the sofa, with him mostly on top.

"Would you like me to come to Toptofty, after work tomorrow and help you set things up? Make sure of the vital things, like that you know where important files are, that nobody has made an appointment during the Works' Holiday, for instance."

"I've got a good secretary, but yes please."

"Are you okay for the moment? Can you let me up, because I really should see to the tea, before it spoils."

"Of course," he said, whilst releasing her: "Even though I don't want to."

"That's nice, to be wanted like that. If you still need me later, you can have me again, I don't mind." Maud rose as Seb sat back up and examined her housecoat. She took it off and dried her breasts with it, then went through to prepare the tea wearing only her slippers and a delicately patterned pair of gauzy bikini briefs. On her way she threw the housecoat into the washing basket. The view overall, and the way her pert breasts jiggled as she walked, did nothing whatever to soften Seb's rampant manhood.

Tea was eaten in a companionable silence with Seb mostly staring at the middle of his young Aunt's chest, but occasionally swapping smiles with her.

"Have you had sufficient tea?"

"Yes thank you."

"Carry the plates through for me."

Seb watched as she prepared to wash up. He reached out and caressed a shoulder.

"Do you need to hold me again? You can if you want. You can do anything you want, I don't mind."

He slid his hands round her waist and up to play with her breasts, watching himself over her shoulder.

"Yes please. Can I snuggle?"

"Snuggle up tight, wriggle and play. You can have whatever you need, I don't mind."

"I -- I --"

"You can have whatever you want Seb. I don't mind."

When Seb at last took her at her word and caressed across the front of her briefs, she spoke softly to him,

"If there's anything in your way, just take it off."

The briefs rolled half way down her thighs like a rope hobble, before Seb decided he'd created enough space and gingerly began to explore, for him, despite his claims at school, uncharted territory. Whilst throwing a quick tender smile at him over her shoulder, Maud spread for him.

He snuggled up and held her tightly, wriggling against her. From where they were standing, at least half a dozen windows could view them and many more with binocular assistance. Seb took his indifference towards the possibility of being observed from Maud.

He watched the growing pile of draining pots with trepidation.

"Can I come back for more after?"

"You can do anything you need to do, have anything you want. We have two weeks here and another two in Cornwall after that. If you want to spend it playing doll, you can. I'd like that."

"Oh. Oh yes, that would be lovely." He released her and dried the pots as she washed them. Presently there wasn't anything more to do. She took the tea towel from him and turned to hang it up. He slid his arms back around her.

"I normally go to bed at about ten, but tonight we'll do it a bit earlier. Go and put your dirty clothes in the basket and lay your new ones out for tomorrow. Then go and have your shower. I'll finish off in here and come through in a minute."

Sebastian obeyed her, sorting through his laundry and putting out his clothes for the morning on his bed. He'd put them on the chair after his shower. He hadn't even begun to wash his hair when Maud joined him in the shower and began washing him. The water made little pattering sounds on her shower cap. His shock and astonishment utterly failed to influence his gallant reflex, which was immediate and impressive and very embarrassing. Maud merely washed it lovingly, washing the embarrassment away.

"Have you ever done it? Properly, with a girl?"

"No." He croaked.

"Would you like to, with me, now?"

Sebastian only nodded, unwilling to risk his voice again.

"Well, the chances are you won't last long, not the first time. And in that case, would you like your first one in here, now? Then we can take our time in bed, we'll enjoy each other better, when you're not gagging to come."

"Oh Maud."

"Bend forward a little." She slid her arms up round his neck: "Now lift me up." As he straightened up she cuddled her legs onto his hips, gripping him tightly jockey style. "You're not quite in the right place, it's a little further under -- Yes -- Little short strokes until you're right up, then you can cut loose, just, don't drop me when you come."

"Do I have to pull out?"

"Don't you dare! Don't you ever pull out of me, but I'm protected anyway."

Sebastian managed not to drop her, but it was a seriously near miss.

They might have gone to bed early, in the double bed that prior to that evening Sebastian had never dreamed he would ever see the inside of, but they went to sleep late.

The exhausted boy lay sprawled across his Aunt, softly snoring. She gently eased the precautionary little towel out from under her bottom and dropped it on the floor. It was soaked through with the most immediate indications of their pleasure. She tenderly caressed his hair and settled for sleep.

The cards from the family arrived on the Thursday and the letters from Sebastian Senior on the Saturday, one for Seb and one for Maud.

Seb collected them from the front door and returned to bed, opening his and gave his Aunt hers.

He pulled his letter out of the envelope and bounced onto the bed to read it.

And froze.

It began,

My dearest, darling, Maud,

I can't --

Chapter 19

October 1987 -- December 1987

Megan

The primary target of most female undergraduates at Megan's College was to find a husband and she was no exception. She accepted the offer of a date from a second year boy who would fit the bill admirably. When he walked her back home, drew her into a dark corner of her College building and moved smoothly into his routine to prise her out of her knickers, she helped and made sure that the time, effort and money that he'd invested in her, paid a handsome return.

The Fresher went to bed that night dreaming of Honeymoons and Kids and Romance; dreams that lasted a whole twelve hours.

In the Coffee Bar her boy was wedged in a corner, although she could join the table she couldn't get near him. The conversation was light and general for a time and then the forthcoming Halloween Ball came up in discussion. The fancy dress aspect was intriguing and the pros and cons of hiring, DIY and adapting something that could still be worn afterwards, were thoroughly explored. Megan sat bathed in the secure knowledge that she would be going and who with.

"I'd like to go," murmured Peter, a shy, quiet boy from her course: "But I've got nobody to go with."

"Take, Megan," said her boy from across the table. "You get a bloody good shag when you take her home."

Megan rose in the stunned silence, which followed,

"Don't call us and we won't call you," she said, leaned over the table and pushed the water jug over into his lap.

When would she ever learn, she had made the mistake of accepting a date from another Roger.

No, that wasn't fair on Roger, at least he kept his mouth shut. Megan Modale, will you ever learn.

That afternoon in the Geology Laboratory, tentatively, Peter approached her.

"May I apologize to you for that vile insult this morning?"

"No. You didn't insult me."

"But I was implicated by association, I would love to take you to the Halloween Ball and I would not expect any favours afterwards."

"Everyone would know you had received them though, whether you did or not, everyone would know you had."

He drew her away into a corner out of earshot.

"Everyone but us. We would know the truth. I have someone at home. We would be partners at the Ball, nothing else, I wouldn't even snog you afterwards."

"What if I lost it and asked you to?"

"Not even if you wanted me to. You are best friend material, not lover material, not for me, you're the wrong sex."

"Oh -- Oh!"

"And I'd appreciate it if you kept that to yourself."

"Am I a smoke screen?"

"Yes."

"Have you really got someone at home?"

"Oh yes. He's very real."

"Well in that case, I'll accompany you to the ball. If the offer was meant."

"Meant and really pleased about it. What are we going as?"

"Well how about --"

The only down side of the arrangement was that Megan was no longer thought of as available and, for those boys who would have been loyal and considerate, her summary treatment of a callous bully placed her in 'sup with a long spoon' territory.

Megan wasn't too bothered, a husband might have been top of her list, but it was only by a nose, a good degree was right up there alongside.

With a set of very good results in her first assignments behind her, she went home for Christmas happy, confident and with several essays to prepare, and if she could manage it in the time, write.

Chapter 20

December 1987

Ben:

Sixth form proved an idyllic haven for Ben, with Roger having left to work in a racing stable. As Christmas approached, the students began organising parties, the main item on the agenda being the chance to try each other out for snogging. Ben joined in enthusiastically with the organisation, but with little success in the snogging stakes. Boys usually outnumbered girls, occasionally by a substantial margin and the choice was further reduced by most of the latter being paired off anyway. Any free girls were usually snapped up by prowling wolves, before the shy and unsure got themselves going. Those who, despite hating the description, actually believed themselves to be geeks had no chance.

Ben tagged along a poor last.

The only possibility seemed to be for him to bring his own girl with him. Great! Down from The Impossible to merely A Miracle, a breeze.

Then, Megan came home for the holidays.

As soon as their respective parents had left for work the following morning, he forced himself to go next door and invite her to the party being organised that night.

"Okay."

"Oh."

"Don't look so surprised, Ben, you must have thought I might say yes, or you wouldn't have asked."

This was not quite true, Ben had genuinely expected her to say no and Megan must have read it in his eyes.

"You didn't, did you?"

"Well --"

"I'm sick of men who don't treat girls with respect. You always have, so yes, I'll go out with you."

"Oh -- It's a snogging party."

"That's okay, you can snog me with respect and if I like it enough --" She tipped her head, giving him the eyes.

"There will be lots of boys there. Looking for girls to snog."

"If I go with you, I stay with you, as my date. At least for tonight. Don't worry, smile. Thank you for the invite, I'm sure we'll have a lovely time -- Together!"

"Seven-o-clock then?"

"I'll be ready."

Ben went home and began to shake; he felt a little better after he'd been sick.

The pairing was an instant success; the neighbours had always liked each other and thoroughly enjoyed the new aspect to their relationship, snogging each other.

At the party, the bedrooms were in great demand and usually had two or three couples already ensconced. Megan made no objection when he drew her away upstairs and it was she who found the recently vacated, available strip down the edge of a crowded bed.

"I do like it enough --" When her boy failed to up the ante, she added: "Ben if you want to feel me up, you can."

Despite being given permission to play, and wanting to very much, Ben only moved very slowly, it wasn't long before Megan took over and boldly guided him towards his goal.

"There are people watching."

"Ben, you're with me, not people, I would like to be the centre of your attention please." She took his hand and thrust it assertively up her dress, all the way to her knickers. "Feel me please."

Ben obliged.

Soon afterwards, he managed to assist her to remove her knickers before she was forced to ask him to do it.

Ben furtively looked around. In the dim light, he could see the pale vee of Megan's bare thighs above her stockings either side of his caressing hand and his own member being fondled in hers. Other boys glanced about momentarily, but all the girls, some with more on show even than Megan, lay quietly, apart from some wriggling, eyes shut, petting their partners. In a sudden flurry of activity, the boy lying next to them rolled over on top of his girl, snuggled into place and then began thrusting purposefully between her spread thighs, which slowly came up cuddling him. Suddenly, Megan gushed goo all over his fingers,

"Now!" She said in his ear and pulled him over onto her, guiding him in.

"I'll pull out," he murmured back.

"No! Don't! No need. Just do it!" and cuddled his vibrating body to her, vice-like tight.

After a rest, murmured thanks and discouragement from vacating the room, or even moving, he required little urging to deliver a much better performance as an encore.

The third time, back home, standing, with Megan pressed up against the wall in a dark corner in the shadow of her garage, he needed no encouragement whatever to perform to her total satisfaction.

Ben didn't need to ask her, his girl's dead faint in his arms when she came, was comment enough. It was sudden and unexpected and it was a struggle to avoid dropping her, but very gratifying and ego boosting.

Having discovered what all the fuss was about and having decided that there was reason for it, he couldn't wait to get back for more and, under the expert guidance of his mistress, quickly began to please her, several times a day.

His Saturday job in the local Greengrocery Shop became full time for the week before Christmas and that between Christmas and New Year. Unwilling to risk even a moment off guard, in case his place was usurped, he broke the news with trepidation,

"I'll not see you tomorrow, I'm working."

"What about tomorrow night?"

"Oh yes, but--"

"I've got three essays to write, Ben, that's many days hard work. If you're not available, that's all to the good, I can research and write during the day and I won't be tempted to shirk them snogging you. But by seven-o-clock, I'll be ready for a lovely relaxing time with you. If that's all right?"

"Oh yes, seven would be fine. Where would you like to go?"

"Absolutely not bothered. A little walk to somewhere quiet and back, with a long sexy snogging session in between?"

"Fine, I think we can manage that."

Predictably, Ben was seen as easy opposition and Megan obviously way out of his league. Several serious attempts to prise the older girl away were made at Christmas and New Year parties, while Ben was getting drinks, or fetching food. Ben caught sight of the first through a doorway and Megan's summary treatment of the interloper. Thereafter he carefully failed to notice, or comment on, fresh cigarette burns on the backs of hands, or an apparent case of incontinence that any horse would have been proud of, he just replaced the drained glasses with fresh pints.

The sessions blossomed from enjoyable sex, to tender love-making and Ben told himself that he genuinely didn't mind that he wasn't her first. He carefully blotted out of his mind a precise name that might have had that honour, repeating to himself that it was none of his business whom she shagged before him.

Presently he even began to deceive himself into thinking that he had accepted it.

The sixth former knew enough about sex to know the possible outcome and once he accepted that merely snogging him was not a nightly option in Megan's eyes, had again offered to jump off. The undergraduate reassured him,

"I take a rather unusual little Smartie each night, we're fine, keep going. Don't ever jump off me, Ben, there's no need and, even if there was, I'd rather you got me pregnant, than spoil the nicest thing anyone has ever done to me."

Chapter 21

January 1988

Mary

When the cleaning of the Library job ended and Mary's appearances at the Rectory became sporadic and then only when a specific job needed doing, Nigel began making Pastoral calls at the Andrew house and expressing his regret when he discovered that, yet again, Grandma had just gone out.

"I felt sure that I would catch her this time. Don't tell her, Mary, we don't want to upset her, that she missed me."

"I won't," she stood aside to let the Curate in. "Would you like a cup of tea?"

"No, in case she comes back, I'll tell you a story first then if Grandma comes back, she can give me the tea."

The Curate sat on the sofa and Mary sat on his lap snuggling herself down onto him.

The story about a Highwayman abducting a maidservant and riding off with her astride his horse had Mary as excited as when she rode Teddy.

Nigel grunted and shook and jerked about.

When he took his leave of her, she went upstairs and rode Teddy until she fell off him.

Presently, Mary could predict when Nigel would appear.

January 1988: Mary

When her Grandma got ready to go to town, or to the shops, or an extended clean through at the Rectory, Mary would tidy up and change into something comfortable, ready to ride the young Curate off into the sunset.

She was rarely wrong.

When he was caught celebrating New Year, with one of Mary's classmates, efforts were made to interview Mary too.

Grandma put her foot down.

Without consulting Mary, she announced that he had never been in the house and refused to take part in any further discussion on the matter.

The Church Authorities, anxiously pursuing damage limitation, were only too glad to accept a story that they must have known was untrue and withdraw gracefully.

Chapter 22

January 1988 -- July 1988

Ben

School restarted after the New Year and Megan departed south at the same time. Although she hadn't spoken about relationships, her conversation included the name of a boy on her course often. Ben suspected he already knew and decided he had to have it confirmed.

"Is there a special boy at College?"

"No."

"Peter? You talk about him a lot."

"He's lovely and a very good friend, my best friend at College. But he has a boy back home too. You have nothing to fear from Peter."

"Oh -- Oh!"

"It's me that's scared -- That you'll find someone else, while I'm gone. Do you think you might? I'll be back late March." Ben took her face in his hands,

"You have nothing to be scared of. Even if I went looking, I know I wouldn't find and I have no reason to go looking. I've got what I want, if you'll come back to me?"

"Oh I'll do that all right. You have a deal Mr Brown. Would you like to do something to me now, that I'll remember, that will keep me going until March?"

During the Spring Term, the weekly letters and telephone calls became very hot and explicit and the Easter Vacation was over, before they had tried half the interesting activities they had discussed, whilst several dozen miles apart.

On their last night before Megan returned to College,
"I'll be going on an archaeological dig after the exams. It's part of the course, but I've heard that they can become shagathons, so I've asked Peter if I can share a tent with him. It will keep the wolves off my back and the man-eaters off his and I'll be kept chaste and safe for you. He often quotes that famous comedian's comment on vagina's, you know at birth he claims to have thought--"
"That's the last time I'm ever going up one of those! Okay, I'll entrust you to Peter's tender care and not worry. Meanwhile do you want something special to keep you going until July?"
"Yes please."

* * *

As June slid into July and it seemed never to get dark, Ben curbed his impatience for the return of his love. But her first night home found him on the doorstep, with flowers.
"Oh -- Thank you, they're lovely."
Megan was ready and Ben only had to wait for a few moments while she stood the bouquet in water for later, took a tablet and washed it down with more water.
"What was that?"
"Antibiotics." She showed him the healing scar. "That cut I got on my hand, while I was on the dig. I didn't want to worry you, so I didn't tell you, but it got infected, so you'll have a cheap night, I can't drink while I'm on these."
"Are you sure it's all right?"
"Yes worry-boots, that's why didn't tell you, it's nothing. It's getting better, I'll be off them in a few days.

Ben and Megan crept round from behind her house and checked their clothes by the still warming up street-light. Apart from her lacy panties sticking out of her handbag, an error they rectified immediately, everything seemed to be in order.

"Tomorrow, jeans and mountain shirt, walking boots and cag. I have a surprise for you and we are going on a picnic."

"Oh." Ben's lack of enthusiasm for the project was both tangible and prickly.

"And when we come home, you can apologize for the glum face and tell me how much you enjoyed it."

"I will enjoy being with you, but not avoiding dripping ice-creams, screaming kids, nor swatting wasps or other wildlife."

"Have you been taking your vitamin B tablets?"

"Yes, since Easter, like you told me."

"Then the only wildlife you'll have to worry about is me. All the wasps are Ichneumonidae, the kids have horns and we will only see some if we are very lucky and if the ice cream drips, I'm sure you won't mind."

She smiled wickedly at his astonished eyes and disappeared into her home.

The following day dawned bright and calm. By breakfast time, the ground hugging mist had been burned off and the temperature was climbing.

Megan met him at her gate with a cool-box,

"Well the weather could melt the ice cream, I grant you," she said: "Would you get the drinks please." She was waving at another box, still on her step.

Ben obediently carried the other box out; Megan had already climbed into the driver's seat. Ben stopped, gawping.

"Get in. This is the surprise. I passed my test last month, we're mobile. Well sort of, when I can prise a car out of somebody."

"Is the picnic just us?"

"Yes."

"Oh, it's suddenly become potentially enjoyable."

Megan drove out westwards from Novochester, until she crossed the North Tyne and then struck out in a more northerly direction. Ben was following her track on the four miles to an inch map, when suddenly she turned right, over a cattle grid and climbed up a steep farm track.

"We're off this map. Well I mean we're still on the map, but--"

"But this road isn't marked."

"Yes. It's 'Here be Dragons' from now on."

"Not in here." Megan tapped her forehead: "I'm still in my own back yard. Well cousin Betty's back yard really, but I know a few of the nooks."

"Nookey nooks?" asked Ben hopefully.

"What do you think?"

Presently, Megan breasted a rise and rolled the car to a halt on a piece of hard standing with seriously muscular snowploughs parked neatly to one side.

"Look hard." She handed him a pair of binoculars and pointed to the cliff walls a quarter of a mile away: "That's where the kids are, but you need good eyes to see them."

Ben stared at her for a moment then put the binoculars to his eyes.

Just blurred green and grey.

He turned the knurled knob and the cliff face jumped sharply into focus.

Neither kids, nor adults. No grandmothers in bath chairs, not that he had expected any.

Of babes in pushchairs there were none.

He panned slowly across the rocks.

A large grey goat looked angrily straight into the lens.

"Goats! Well one goat -- It's got four horns -- They're huge!"

"You are looking at one of the district's best kept secrets. Wild goats. Well feral goats really, they escaped when Henry VIII razed the local monasteries to the ground in the Sixteenth Century. Impressive aren't they?"

"They are. There's three of them -- They've gone -- I didn't see them go, they've just gone."

Megan started the car,

"Yes they do that, you'll not see them again. You were very lucky."

"You didn't see them."

“It’s okay, I’ve seen them before, when I came up and stayed with Betty.”

Trees closed in all around them as the outposts of the 'biggest man-made forest in Europe' coalesced into the main event. Presently, Megan slowed on the crest of a sudden sharp rise. The track joined a poorly maintained forest road. The heavy usage was obviously a right turn, a hundred metres or so down to a smoothly metalled forest highway, the access to which was barred by a stout pole barrier.

“We can’t get out,” said Ben pointing.

“That’s to keep the tourists from getting lost in the forest,” said Megan: “The locals, and me, know ways round the barriers.” She turned left, onto the section heavily overgrown with grass and weeds.

“Not long now, to the Snake.”

Grouse began to appear.

“There must be a heather moor close by, for grouse.”

“Just over there.” She nodded ahead and to their left: “Bollyfaith Moss, deadly place, Northumberland’s black hole, full of bodies and off road bikes, the odd aircraft -- We’re here.”

Ahead was a river valley, barely a long cricket-ball throw wide. The tiny river flowing in it, did so in incongruously big meanders. The bank they were on sloped gently downwards. At the bottom the poorly maintained road, which by now had degenerated into a grassy track, took a sharp left turn. It crossed the river via a concrete slab bridge and disappeared up the much steeper far side, doubling back out of sight among trees, vaguely in the general direction of Bollyfaith Moss.

Megan ran the car off the road, down a shallow incline towards the tiny river. She was following a pair of thin earth strips just visible among the vegetation. The strips of earth turned right, in the upstream direction, across a wide flat lawn and disappeared under the concrete slab bridge.

“If it was wet, I’d not dare this bit in anything but a 4x4 but it will be fine today.” She executed a neat three-point turn and parked up facing back the way they had come.

Together the pair spread out a rug, on the short lush grass, between the car and the bridge and stood the lunch box on it.

"Sit down," she said indicating the rug. "No, just sit down and say nowt. I brought us here for a reason." She moved away slightly, to the broad concrete slab base of the bridge.

"You might want to loosen your trousers. Well the idea is that you will need to. I hope!"

Obediently, Ben, now suspecting what she had in mind, loosened his trousers and took them off.

"I take it we are not likely to be disturbed?"

"That's why here. It's very unlikely, but if we are, they are going to get an eyeful."

Megan began to hum tunes, mainly variations on 'The Stripper,' and slowly, sexily, peeled her clothes off at the same time. She started at the inside with her bra and knickers and worked outwards, giving Ben tantalising glimpses of what wasn't underneath her top and skirt from time to time and glanced occasionally at his rapidly tenting underpants.

Ben too removed the rest of his clothes leaving the tent until last.

Megan, now naked, approached him, undulating her hips and shimmying her shoulders, as he, entranced, peeled his last garment off.

"Wow," she said: "First objective achieved. Second one coming up."

She knelt astride and together they guided him into her. Smiling she entwined her fingers in his, pushed his arms above his head and began to ride him, like a pony in an alternating little bob, long stroke pattern.

"Is -- that -- ni -- ?" She tried to ask but her eyes rolled as she melted down onto him and he had to take over and trigger the now familiar, and expected, dead faint.

A few minutes later she spoke without moving,

"That was lovely, thank you."

"Oh! I didn't know you were back with me. Thank you, you thought it up. But you're right it was lovely."

"You had never seen me properly. I wanted you to see **me**, properly. See me all over, enjoy **me**!"

"I did and it was lovely, you are lovely."

"In a little while I want you to break out the picnic and use me as the plate. Set the food out on me and then feed me and eat it off me and when you can't stand it any more climb on and do me, do me and do me until -- Well just do me!"

"Three times in one day again and you didn't want to come and avoid dripping ice-creams."

"I was wrong. Licking chocolate ice-cream off your nipples was well worth coming for. But you were wrong too, it wasn't three it was four. The last two were back to back off the same stand. I'm really proud of myself for that."

"That explains it, I was coming for ages. Thank you, thank you, thank you."

"Thank you!"

At the end of the picnic they cleaned themselves up with baby-wipes that Megan had brought specially.

"You've made me as horny as ever."

Ben's spirit was more than willing, but,

"I'm sorry darling, but you can see, he's as much use as a dead ferret."

"Would you rub me then? It won't take long I'm nearly there already."

Ben kissed his way down her tummy whilst stroking her, waiting for a horrified reaction, ready instantly to change course if he got it.

Megan tenderly stroked his hair and her murmurs of,

"Oh, Ben -- Yes, please -- Darling, Ben," gained a pleading quality.

Confident now, he homed in on his target and not knowing any better tried some sucking licks.

Megan had been correct, she was already nearly there, she promptly exploded.

They packed up the sad remains of their feast and while Megan folded the rug, Ben went to explore. He stepped onto the concrete slab that his girl had used as her stage, peering into the darkness under the bridge.

"Did you know this track goes under the bridge?"

"Yes, but that's all it does. It doesn't come out the other side. I think it used to at one time, but there's a culvert thing in the way now."

Ben disappeared under the bridge; then his voice came back out, booming with resonance,

"So there is."

Chapter 23

June 1988 -- August 1991

Sebastian

Maud drew her letter out of the envelope,

Son,

I hope you're your being good for your Aunt,

She looked across at Sebastian, he proffered the other letter, wooden faced.

"I think I've got yours."

Maud looked at the greeting,

"Ah. Two plus two doesn't always make four, Sebastian, but in this case it does. I'll tell you anything you want to know. Just ask."

Breakfast was eaten in a polite silence, which continued during the washing up. Maud broke it,

"Come and sit beside me on the sofa. I'll tell you anything you want to know." They sat down. "I'd like to hold your hand,

I'm not going to find this easy." Sebastian took her hand, entwining her fingers.

"Do you love him?"

"Yes."

"Are you going to break them up?"

"No. I love my sister too and I'm not a home wrecker."

"Does Mum know?"

"I'm sure she does. She's never asked. When your Dad comes to see me, or we go out, she pointedly never asks. I've been with your Dad on dozens of business trips. Trips she knew all about. She's even booked our room for us occasionally."

"Why? I mean, why everything?"

"Your Dad was in the Scouts, I was in the Brownies. I fell for him completely. Asked him out, took him home. Your Mum fell for him too. He could date a sixteen year old, not get into legal hassle when she invited him into her bed. I'd already done that, but he wisely turned a seven year old down."

"Mum had me when she was seventeen."

"Your Dad is a good catch. Your Mum is a lot of things, but stupid she ain't. If she didn't bag him for us, someone else would. She could do it, so she did, I went along with it. We sort of discussed it. Just a couple of sentences.

'Do you really want him?'

'Yes.'

'So do I. Share?'

'Okay.' So when I swarmed onto your Dad's lap, or took him upstairs to show him my dolls, she looked the other way. Even covered for us sometimes."

"What about me?"

"I've loved you since you were born. When I baby-sat you, when you were little, I used to bathe you with me. I had to stop because I wanted to do more than just bathe you. Now you're old enough, I can bathe you again, not strangle the love I have for you."

"Does Dad know about us?"

"I'm sure he does--"

"You said that about Mum knowing, when the right answer was a simple yes."

"Yes. Like your Mum, we haven't really discussed it, but he must know how I feel about you, I've never made any secret of it. When your Mum insisted you stay with me, he just said, 'Now's your chance to look after him.' I took that to mean any way I thought fit. I didn't know how to start and then you came home needing comfort and support. That I'm good at."

"So where do we go from here?"

"If you'd like to share me with your Dad, like I share your Dad with your Mum, I'd agree to that. I'd quite like it. Someday you'll meet a girl of your own and I'll lose you. But, meanwhile I can enjoy you. Think about it. I'm going shopping, tell me when I come home."

"I'd rather share, than not have you at all."

"It's only a two option choice."

The new couple made sure that they set out on holiday before the rest of the family returned.

* * *

Apart from the lurid illuminated sign reading;

SEX SHOP

the frontage was conservative and understated.

"Come on, I like seeing what's available," said Maud towing him towards it. "I tend to stay away from those at home because I don't want people to know how I feel about sex. People generally are prudes; sex is black or white, no shades of grey. I see myself as a slightly dark, mid-grey; I don't mind you knowing."

Inside, the selection of goods had Sebastian's senses and sensibilities reeling. Maud waved negligently at the rows of dildoes modelled on ponies.

"Don't bother too much about them," she said: "They're for men to buy because they think that's what we want. Girls don't buy them for themselves."

"What do you buy?"

"These." She led him over to a display of small pads, cushions and fingers. "They're not meant to be pushed inside.

Mostly a girl gets pleasure from being titillated outside, well I do anyway."

"Which one would you like?" He was reaching into his pocket.

"Hang on a bit, lets have a good look round. I promise if there's something I really like, you can buy it for me if it's not expensive."

The couple toured the premises, Sebastian had the usual teenage boys misconceptions; Maud put him right on several more.

"Those huge strap-ons are rubbish. The good ones are those small electric powered ones."

"For two girls?"

"Or more likely for a girl to use on her man." She watched him steadily as the pennies dropped.

"Oh."

"Do you still want to buy me something?"

Sebastian nodded.

"Okay. I'd like this please." She plucked up a cellophane package containing a blindfold, a pierced ball gag and several hanks of thin rope. The rope was Royal Blue, limp and shiny and very soft to the touch.

"What would you want that for?"

"Games. In my job I spend my entire day trying to turn toads into princesses. When frankly most of them look more attractive as toads. Why? Because most of us like to think of ourselves as princesses." She held up the rope. "Tied up and gagged, in the dark, I'm not a beauty consultant any more, I can be anything. Slave girl, captured princess, anything I want to be. Toad, even. And you could do anything you want to me."

"You let me do that now."

"But tied up, I don't have the choice to let you or not. I'd get a big buzz from that."

"Can I get you a vibrator too?"

"The pad. The one that looks like a baby's sponge, wrung out and bent."

"Okay."

Sebastian found out later that night that he really liked tying Maud up before he had her, and the effect on his Aunt was electrifying. An hour or so spent tied to their bed became a special treat, daily event for her, throughout their holiday.

The day he was due to return home, Sebastian put his cases in Maud's car and returned to take his leave of her.

"Erm --"

"You say thank you and kiss me tenderly. Then I take you home." Obediently he did so and they made the journey largely in silence. As they turned into his street, she mentioned the subject he'd been unable to broach.

"If you want, I'll keep Wednesday free for you."

"Yes please."

"Every Wednesday you come for tea and an evening of talk with your Aunt. Be completely open about being with me--"

"And silent on the details of what we do together."

"Yes."

Sebastian was consumed with the desire to mention his father, but managed not to do so. It took months more, but eventually he managed to accept that, just as he had a life with Maud totally private to them, so had his Dad and to respect the privacy.

Chapter 24

August 1988

Roger, Sarah

Doing your two in a training stables is a hard demanding job, which relies on selfless commitment and dedication to the welfare of other people, who just happen to be horses, as much on giving fair return for your hire.

After one week in the job, Roger knew it was not what he wanted for a career.

After one year, he was desperately looking for a way out.

The 'lads', three of whom were girls, were talking about their futures one night. Roger, unusually, did a lot of listening, rather than talking.

"It's just that these days there's not much else except racing," said a grizzled oldster, the Dad of the lads by some decades: "When I was young, every firm that delivered anything had horses. Brewers, milk, rag and bone men."

"Farmers? Or had tractors come in by then?"

"Oh no. There were more horses than tractors. I hadn't seen a tractor when I was your age. There were more horses than cars. A car in the street was an event. A horse, every day, usually several times a day."

"But I see lots of horses in the fields, when I'm on holiday."

"Thousands, hundreds? Twenty? When I was a kid I'd see more than twenty on my way home from school."

"Oh."

"So what is open to us besides ladding? Those of us that are too big for jockeys? Me, Sarah -- Roger."

"Show jumping if you're good enough, Sarah's good enough."

"But no money. It's a rich girl's sport," the good enough girl argued.

"Marry one of those morning coated la-las whose tongues drag on the floor when they see you. Make it a business deal, arranged marriage thing. He can have free access to that lot." Dad nodded at Sarah's impressive goodies, concealed as usual behind rough stable clothes. "In return for your free access to his money. I'd go for it, if I had money and in my case you wouldn't have long to wait before you were free again. And rich too. But get it in writing first, then married, then access to the goodies!"

"And if all else failed you could always get him to wear a fur coat and, like, close your eyes."

"Tried that, Roger," said Sarah into the shocked silence: "Remember, when you got me drunk on Valentine's night. For a man you're okay, but you're not as big as a horse and at your level of performance, size matters."

"Now listen b--"

"Enough!" barked the older man: "You were gratuitously offensive to a girl who'd let you sample the goodies and she shot your head off. I'd have shot your balls off, so shut it."

"Years ago you could have been a highwayman, or a bounty hunter in America's Old West," said another of the lads, straight at Roger's eyes: "But I don't think you have the self discipline for the Life Guards, or Mounted Police." He turned to the attractive girl: "Now, Sarah about this agreement that Dad mentioned. I've got a Nat West Pig, which isn't empty, so what if --"

The conversation became gentle teasing of the girls, as to exactly what any of them would swap for a Poke in a Pig, or even a-for-a.

August 1988: Roger, Sarah

Roger forced himself to calm down by musing on one of the options that had been ruled out for him. Being a Mounted Policeman would have distinct side advantages.

At a race meeting a couple of weeks later,

"Who's the chinless wonder Sarah's, like, making a play for?"

"I don't blame her one jot, she loves horses, not men, I think--"

"I know all that, I don't blame her either as it happens, but, like, who is it?"

"Freddie Botchitt, younger son of the Earl of Stumfordham, there's certainly plenty of money there."

Sarah wasn't making a play for Freddie at all, she was investigating the reactions of the brother of a friend to her long term plans for her future. Plans that would significantly involve both the friend and her brother.

"I have no objections," said Freddie, "I think it's a great idea."

"Could you have a quiet word with Lady Anne for me? Test the water there too. I'll speak to her about it myself as soon as I see her, but it might be easier if she already knows what I'm planning."

"She's here, somewhere, you'll be busy, you've got horses entered. I'll let her know, I'm sure she'll want to come down to discuss it."

Sarah's horse won it's race, a moderate ranked Hurdle event, but greeted with joy by the stable lads who had all backed it. Smiling and deeply pleased, Sarah led her horse back from the unsaddling enclosure to the stables.

"Sarah!"

The stable 'lad' turned from congratulating her charge to greet the girl hurrying towards her.

"Lady Anne, Viscount Freddie said you were here."

The girls kissed and hugged.

"He's told me about your ideas, I came straight over to discuss them in more detail."

"Oh, you don't mind then?"

"Mind? I think it's a great idea, really, all I want to know is how far you are prepared to go?"

"For the right deal, total commitment. The centre of my Universe."

"How about wife?"

"That's what I'd really want, truth be told, it's just that there's the age gap. He might not--"

"It's not a problem, he defended Sir William on exactly that issue only last week. Look, how about I speak to him and you come for the weekend. I'll prepare the ground, then you can put your case."

"Would you? That sounds nice, I'll ask Dad if he'll do my two, we've covered for each other before, I should be able to come."

Back home in the stables, with their charges seen to and settled for the night, Sarah spoke to the oldster,

"Dad could you possibly do my two, this weekend, Saturday and Sunday? I'll pay you back next week."

"Where are you going?"

"Castle Greenewell."

"The Country Seat of the Earl of Stumfordham, Young Freddie Botchitt a serious target then?"

"No not Freddie, he's totally elsewhere, I'm aiming much higher."

"His mother died a couple of years ago, I hear the Earl's only now getting over it."

"Is that a fact?" asked Sarah, tossed her head and turned away to pack her bag for the weekend. "I must ask after his health."

Lady Anne Botchitt met Sarah at the door of her Ancestral Home, the following Friday,

"Sarah, you're looking well."

"Lady Anne, I am thank you and you are blooming."

The girls kissed.

"I look good I grant you, but this morning sickness thing is the pits. Come in, I'll take you to your room and you can freshen up."

"Have you managed to speak with the Earl at all?"

"Oh, yes. He listened and agreed to let you put your proposition to him."

"Oh, thank you."

"I'm actually hoping quite intently that you'll be able to drop the 'Lady' before Sunday Lunch."

"Oh, yes. That would be nice."

At a few minutes before seven, Sarah, now freshly bathed and dressed appropriately, entered the drawing room, walked straight over to Lady Anne's father and introduced herself,

"Good evening My Lord. I'm Sarah, I'm a friend of Lady Anne's from University. I visited once, but we only met briefly."

"Nevertheless I remember you. You showed the Countess how to plait a mane, it was one of the best of the last days. I've always been grateful to you for that, but never thanked you. Would you take a turn in the Japanese Garden with me, there's a few minutes before dinner."

The Earl offered his arm and the pair walked out through the French windows. Behind them, the next generation exchanged smiles, with enlightened eyes.

"So a formal thank you for pleasing my wife so deeply just a week before she died."

"I enjoyed doing it. She was so nice to me and an eager pupil. I was glad I could do something....." Sarah tailed off into silence, confused and now it had come to the crunch, embarrassed.

The Earl patted her hand,

"And now you want to progress in your career. You have the talent, but you lack the funds required."

"Succinctly put, My Lord."

"I have the necessary disposable income, but not the talent, nor the inclination, I might add." Again he patted her hand in reassurance, "I understand that you are open to business negotiations, where my millions and your very obvious natural attributes could be pooled, to our mutual benefit."

"An apt and accurate description, My Lord."

"And exactly how far would you be prepared to pool your assets."

"For a say equal to yours in the distribution of the millions; up to and including wife and mother of any more of your children."

"You've thought this through, I am thinking?"

"Oh, yes. **And** the need to tell you this before we come to any agreement. I'm not virgin My Lord, three times not virgin and, naturally, there are boys out there that know that."

"Oh, virginity is a vastly over-rated condition, demanded by the Establishment for the Spouse of the Heir Presumptive, purely for their own satisfaction. I'm not virgin either, my dear, and nor was Grace, the Countess, when we first met. It is not an issue, anything else?"

"No, My Lord, nothing comes to mind." The relief in Sarah's voice was obvious to both.

"Very well then, I would like to conclude our negotiations and go into dinner. Miss Sarah Jones, will you marry me?"

"I will My Lord, gladly."

"Soon?"

"Yes, how soon is soon?"

"Give your notice at the stables, then pack. Be ready to move at two minutes notice, you're jumping from nonentity to Gossip-Column-Fodder overnight. I did the Society bit for my first marriage and Grace and I hated both it and the Media Circus around it. I'd rather go Special Licence within the month this time, unless you want the splash do?"

"Special Licence within the month suits me fine, the Media Circus I'd gladly avoid. I never dreamed of Fairytale Romances; Weddings scrutinised by the Media; Parading solely to boost often quite unpleasant people's ambitions; but only of winning Badminton."

"And together we will realize se that dream. I have business in town this weekend and Brussels calls for the next two weeks, so I'm leaving here tonight. Stay here for the weekend as you planned. Put your notice in on Monday. Get packed, passport and everything ready. When the reporters descend on you, smile politely, but say nothing. They will hound you quite roughly and have microphones everywhere, so say **nothing**, just escape with decorum. Once we are married we can make them back off. I'll send you your air-tickets by Secure Mail. We'll get married in Carcassonne, I much prefer the South of France, and Honeymoon in the Pyrenees. Does that sound reasonable to you?"

"Very reasonable, I love mountains, I was one once in a previous reincarnation."

Edward Botchitt snorted with surprised laughter,

"Bring the Tattersalls' Sales Catalogues with you. We'll pick up the French and German ones over there. Right let's go in and shock the servants and, of course, the Great Aunt."

Sarah returned from her weekend and resumed her work, but was quietly replaced a fortnight later. Just before the yard was besieged by reporters.

A month later, there was a photograph in one of the national glossies, Horsewoman And Hunting, of The Earl and new young Countess of Stumfordham buying Event horses.

A year after that, the brilliant young Countess won her first Three Day Event.

Chapter 25

August 1988

Megan

Two weeks after Ben's first celebratory, re-uniting fumble up Megan's skirt, her period failed to arrive.

Every day, girls of child-bearing age, who are also on the pill, get prescribed antibiotics. Some of them get warned about the latter negating the contraceptive effects of the former. Unfortunately, Megan was one of the many that don't.

Six weeks after she returned home, Ben was sure enough of his facts, to ask,

"I've been doing some counting. Shouldn't you have had a period by now?"

"I should have had two. I've missed before, so it was no big deal, but I am being sick in the morning. I've been sick every morning since the first one didn't arrive. I should be okay, but I've been wondering--"

"We are going to see a doctor, useless worrying about whether there is anything to worry about or not."

"I said wonder, not worry, if I am, it will be inconvenient but lovely. And if I am, before you ask, it is yours."

"I wasn't going to ask."

* * *

"Ben it was your decision to visit the doctor. Don't be so nervous. If it's no, there's no problem. If it's yes, it's a weekend problem, but a lifetime's joy."

The bluff, friendly family-doctor, GP, but with a special interest in paediatrics, examined her enthusiastically, when he heard the reason for the visit.

"Did you have an orgasm?"

"Erm -- Well--"

"If you have an orgasm, it bumps any eggs that may be waiting, onwards down the tube to meet any sperm swimming the other way."

"Yes she did doctor, she always does."

"Do you think you jumped off in time?"

"I didn't jump off. Megan's on the pill."

"But I've got a note here about your University Doctor prescribing you a broad spectrum antibiotic, for a seriously infected cut."

"Yes."

"Let me guess, nobody warned you?"

"Warned me about what?"

The Doctor explained about what and was forthright in his opinion,

"-- I knew when you walked in the door. Tests this early are a bit iffy, but take it from me, you're glowing with health, about six weeks pregnant and my guess is, it's a girl. I'm so confident that I'm putting you on the programme now, even before we get --"

Ben Brown had his fair share of faults, but lack of bottle wasn't one of them. He proposed, brushed aside her reservations until she accepted him, whereupon he marched in and told their flabbergasted and irate parents.

"Mum, Dad, can you come next door for a minute?"

When the populace was assembled,

"Er, we're very sorry about this, we didn't plan it this way, but I've accidentally got Megan pregnant, we're going to get married as soon as we can, preferably very soon and we'd like to live with you until we can find a place of our own."

He then calmly shut all the agro out, took Megan aside and began meticulously to plan their future together. Their respective Dads sat open mouthed; Megan's Mum was just about to ask after her daughter's health, when Mrs Brown exploded,

"What do you mean? How did this happen? Wh--"

"Most likely the usual way Muriel, no more of that," said Mr Brown softly.

"It wasn't supposed to happen, but nobody warned me about antibiotics messing with the pill."

"We are sorry, but it's damage limitation now. Megan and I are going to work out our money. We'd be most grateful if you four can think up ways to help us." He took Megan's hand and led her out of the room.

Chapter 26

August 1988 -- September 1991

Ben

The fact that Ben's girl was experienced created at least the possibility of there being a cuckoo in his nest. Faithful to his first statement on the matter, he never mentioned the suspicion to her. In due course he was rewarded for his tact, when she proudly, and with love, presented him with a small, female and beautiful, but otherwise unmistakable clone of himself.

"She's got nothing of mine, not even her sex, because your X is responsible for that too." She commented to him, ruefully.

In town, a year later, with the little one in a pushchair, when she was struggling to open a shop door, Megan found it plucked inwards from her grasp and herself being ushered in by Roger. Whilst revealing only that he was joining the Police, Roger quickly discovered that she had had to transfer to the local Polytechnic to finish her degree, who the father of her baby was and who her husband was.

"What the hell did you, like, marry him for?"

"He's Leanne's father and he asked me to."

"He's got nothing to offer you. I'd have married you, rather than, like, waste yourself on him."

"But I wouldn't have married you, Roger, he's just as good in bed, he's got a good job for a youngster, with prospects and he loves me. Which you don't! Bye."

Megan had made no attempt at confidentiality, and the exchange was witnessed, and reached Ben by several roundabout routes. Having distilled the essence of the story from the differing versions, he came to a fair approximation of the truth, but wondered why Megan hadn't mentioned it.

"Why didn't you tell me you'd seen Roger?"

"He was rude about you and I had to slap him down. It upset me and I thought it might upset you, I could think of no good reason to tell you about something of no consequence, merely to upset us."

Ben's progress through the Apprentice School at Bentwistle Electronics was very fast track, compared with his less able colleagues. It wasn't until he was promoted to Junior Management and had to work alongside his intellectual equals, that his progress slowed and he began, occasionally, to struggle.

When Megan qualified as a teacher however, their combined income and prospects, allowed the purchase of a small house and some luxuries like a cheap, robust-but-thirsty domestic jeep.

Chapter 27

June 1989 -- June 1991

Roger

Roger's advancement through the ranks of the Police was slow rather than spectacular. Far from them welcoming an experienced-beginner horseman recruit into the Mounted Section; they refused to even consider him for the massive waiting list before he'd completed his basic training. His career hadn't been helped either by him accidentally impregnating another youngster, on the initial training course.

When she told him, straight out and up front, in the middle of a shopping mall, Roger looked wildly around him, there were people close by, but nobody overtly listening.

"How the hell did that happen?"

"Well I think what you did to me behind the gym, that night you filled me up with vodka, just might have something to do with it."

"Don't pretend you didn't want it."

"I was out of my skull. You can tell me what I wanted, you can tell me anything, I can't argue, I have no memory of it. But somebody got my cherry that night and Margaret and John both say it was you, so what are you going to do about it?"

"You'll have to get rid of it."

The big man that had been standing with his back to the couple, studying the cameras in a nearby shop window, turned towards them,

"Are you sure you want anything more to do with this cretin?"

"Roger, can I introduce my Dad?"

She had to leave, of course, and her father quietly delivered an ultimatum, which meant Roger married her shortly after. The young wife and mother then showed a strong stubborn streak, when he tried to force hop around the country, chasing after possible promotions. She refused to move, correctly assessing that her husband's average ability was the stumbling block, not the lack of opportunity.

Young Mrs Redcombe had her second child as soon as possible after the first and shortly after that, set about getting herself fit again, to reapply to the Police.

Chapter 28

July 1989

Mary

The young Careers Officer was having a bad first day. His high-pitched voice and affected manner had done him no favours with the first three lads he'd interviewed. From then on he was a poofter and treated accordingly. Late in the afternoon, he'd taken his ire out on the shy retiring mouse that was his last interviewee.

"Name?" He interrupted her reply, as soon as he heard enough to confirm it was the girl next on his list. "What do you want to be?"

"I want to go to Secretarial College."

He glanced up at the plain, dowdy and diffident figure in front of him.

"And study--"

"No you won't do there at all. Domestic service, or cleaner, that's about your mark. This card has the address of your local job centre. There's plenty of cleaning jobs. That will be all."

Outside in the corridor, Mary stared at the blurred card through her tears.

"What's the matter pet?" The other Careers Officer was calling to her from across the corridor.

"I wanted to go to College and train to be an Office Manager, but I have to be a cleaner."

"Come into my room, I'm Norma." She sat the girl down and provided tissues. "It's often difficult to see the way forward pet, but if you want to go to College it will take a lot of hard work. You need five 'A' to 'C's to get into a secretarial course, it's not impossible, just very hard."

"But I've got nine. I'm doing A Levels. Even if I do really badly I'll get Bs, really badly. I'm going for As."

Norma did an exaggerated double take, but when the girl obviously hadn't seen it, she provided another handful of tissues.

"What did Gerald say when you told him that?"

"I didn't tell him. I said I wanted to go to College and he said I had to be a Cleaner."

"Just a minute pet." Norma left. Mary heard her knock on the other door, then use her key, apparently Gerald had gone. She re-appeared a few minutes later holding some forms, the top one of which was the one Mary had filled out prior to her interview. "What is your name?"

"Mary Andrew."

Norma perused the form as she sat down. Ashamed that her tears had been witnessed, Mary fought for and was back in control, by the time Norma spoke again.

"It says you write children's stories."

"Some, a few are my own. The others are based on stories that were told to me as a child, I've changed them a bit, adapted them. I do it to practice my typing, as well as write a story."

Norma ran a sheet of paper into her typewriter, turned the writer round and pushed it over,

"Run me off a story, now."

"Any story?"

"One of yours, not an adaptation, one that's completely yours." She waved at the cable: "It's an electric writer, you only need to touch the keys." Mary nodded, thought for a moment and then poised her hands over the keyboard. She picked the title out briskly, but carefully, gauging the speed and sensitivity of the machine and hit a couple of carriage returns.

Then she took off, machine-gunning the story into print.

Norma walked round to read it over her shoulder. The story concerned eight-year-old Amy who went to the Supermarket to buy a tin of beans, but at the checkout discovered that, by mistake, she had bought an elephant instead. Satisfied, Norma stopped her at the end of the page.

"That'll do pet. I'll keep the job centre card if you don't mind, this folder tells you all you need to know about Secretarial College." She placed it into the girl's hands. "If you apply now, for September next year, my guess is you'll have a provisional place before Christmas. You know, subject to your results."

"Oh. Thank you."

"That's okay. All part of the service."

"Thank you."

"Can I ask, do you always do what people tell you?"

"Yes, I must be polite."

"In future check first, make sure it's the right thing to do."

"Oh."

"And another thing, I couldn't have a copy of Amy's Elephant could I? My daughters would love to read it."

Chapter 29

December 1991 -- April 1992

Sebastian

"Come on Seb, it's Christmas, cheer up!" said the Senior Salesman and drained his glass.

"It's the Christmas Party, Christmas is next week."

"It's leg over time anyway, come on let's split up a pair of girls and make their night."

Sebastian was quite amenable to that idea, only lacking in the technique; it had required no talent to fall onto Maud, she'd done the tripping and beat him to the carpet handsomely. Eagerly, he watched and learned. Several pairs of girls edged past them round the dance floor.

"What's wrong with them?" He asked, as the third pair eased out of range.

"Those girls are all looking for husbands, not for a wild night, these two are looking for bullies to order them about, make them obey and debase themselves. That can be fun occasionally, but it's a wild night I'm after."

So that's what it is, Seb thought. He was familiar with their submissive attitude; they had the same look about them as Aunt Maud. But for the first time he recognised it for what it was.

"I wouldn't mind a girl who wanted to ob--"

"Now here's a wild night, but she's with a dealer." The approaching typists were quite different. The attractive, interesting one was plainly dressed, her clothes were clean, but far from new, not quite shabby, whilst the extraordinarily pretty one dazzled.

"That's okay, anything will do." He hadn't finished speaking by the time Mike had dragged him over to the pair.

"Excuse me, this is Seb, I'm Mike."

"Nonie."

"Margaret."

"Can we cut in please girls?"

To his astonishment, after the polite, polished, pause in proceedings, Sebastian found himself dancing with the dazzling one, while the girl with bare legs and clean but well worn shoes, was whisked off towards a dark corner, by the older man.

A minute later the record finished and a slow number replaced it. Mis-reading Nonie's smile and her body language, Seb moved in, allowing his hand to drop onto her bottom,

"I find you very attractive."

Nonie gently but assertively pushed him away,

"So I can feel, but I don't give freebies. I'm not that kind of girl." Seb disengaged and regrouped instantly,

"Oh. Sorry, I didn't mean an--"

"Thank you for the dance?"

"Thank you."

There was a pause as if she expected more that a mere reply and then she'd gone.

"It was nice," he said to the empty space before him.

Neither Mike nor Margaret was anywhere to be seen.

An hour later Sebastian decided to leave, he turned from getting his coat and bumped straight into Nonie Figgis,

"Oh, sorry."

"That's okay. Have you seen Margaret?"

"Not since our dance. I haven't seen Mike since then either."

"They'll be together."

"Yeah. Erm, can I give you a lift?"

"I told you, I don't give freebies -- No? -- Some other time then, thanks, bye."

He watched her go. She'd made him feel vaguely uncomfortable again, as if he had an itch that wouldn't stay in one place to be scratched. If only she was a submissive, looking for someone to obey.

He didn't see Mike until after the New Year.

"Hello there. Did you have a good Christmas?"

"Best ever and New Year."

"She wasn't just a wild night then?"

"No she wasn't, what I didn't tell you was that if the wild night was good enough, I intended it as a deposit on a much longer term commitment."

"How long?"

"I got engaged. We're getting married in the summer. In one night we became best friends. I was looking for a little raver to be my wife. She was looking for a steady income to raise chicks on. We were lucky, we found each other."

"Congratulations."

"It didn't take us long to thrash out the details. It's more like an arranged marriage than a love match, but lots of them become love matches in due course. We're aiming for that."

Shortly after Sebastian's promotion to Sales Manager, rumours began to circulate about the sexual predator on the Management team and that if things didn't improve, action would be taken. The name of the very angry girl at the centre of the gossip was Nonie Figgis. Sebastian was in a total panic. He knew that rumours were always rife, but now that he was Senior Personnel, they were said in his presence.

He stuck his hands firmly in his pockets, no more lusting after youngsters in the typing pool who screamed sexual harassment if you as much as copped a feel. Not that Nonie had screamed at the Christmas party, but she had definitely objected and he had had to back off quickly. He thought he had calmed her down; she'd spoken to him nicely enough afterwards, but perhaps not. For several months he was a pillar of respectability and, when asked, publicly stated that Sexual Harassment was disgraceful and must not be condoned.

Then the eruption, the Board was to meet, to discuss a charge of Sexual Harassment and would Sebastian present himself promptly at ten-o-clock.

He barely made it to the toilet in time and only just from there to the Boardroom. To his astonishment, he was examined by Counsel, as if in court. He answered in a daze.

"Mr Stripe, have you talked with Miss Figgis about this hearing this morning?"

"No, I didn't even know it was this morning until half an hour ago."

"I didn't mean it that way, I meant have you told her, or discussed with her, at any time, what you intend to say this morning?"

"No, should I have done?"

“Not at all. Mr Stripe, at the Christmas Party, did you make overtures of a sexual nature to Miss Figgis.”

“They were perfectly proper overtures.”

“But, of a sexual nature.”

“Yes.”

“What did Miss Figgis reply?”

“To stop, she was not that kind of girl.”

“How many times did she have to tell you?”

“Only once.”

“You fully understood, clearly, that she wanted you to stop?” Sebastian’s need for yet another trip to the toilet was becoming imperative.

“Yes. I understood and I stopped.”

“So we are led to believe Mr Stripe. I have no further questions.”

What?

Another pinstripe suit stood up,

“Come, come, Sebastian, I can call you Sebastian can’t I, we’re both men of the World, we both know all girls say ‘No’ at first, they really mean ‘Yes if you press it.’”

“That’s quite enough Mr. Agnew. Mr Stripe has clearly stated that when Miss Figgis said ‘No’, he fully understood and, unlike your client,--”

What! Interjected Sebastian's thoughts, almost causing him to miss the next phrase,

"--he respected her wishes. Thank you for your assistance in this matter Mr Stripe, you may go."

Sebastian stumbled out into the sunshine. That he was not the subject of the charges and had been called by Nonie Figgis, as a character witness, to testify that her 'No' clearly meant 'No!' had never occurred to him.

That night, in the Supermarket, he bumped into Margaret, or to be more exact her bump. The wild-night girl had wasted no time in beginning to work down her agenda; she must have jumped the wedding gun by many weeks.

"Congratulations, are you happy?" Seb said nodding significantly.

"Yes, very much so."

"I know Mike's bouncing about with a big grin on. And after this morning so am I." He could see Margaret was puzzled. "I thought it was me Nonie was mad at."

"Baby Bouncers! No! Not you, somebody else entirely. He offered her a ton to go to bed with him, she was furious."

"I can understand."

"I don't think you do, she'd asked for a monkey -- She was not going to settle for just the one. With Nonie, it's a commodity. Love, Sex, it's for sale, but the price is governed by how well you treat her. You could have had her for loose change."

"I never knew --"

"I can see that, anyway take care, I think you're going to be a busy boy, starting very soon."

"What?"

But she had already gone, waving over her shoulder.

It was when it was revealed why the Sexual Harassment hearing had been in secret, shrouded in mystery, that Sebastian began to understand her parting shot.

Chapter 30

May 1992

Rachael

Rachael's first interview with Rita should have been terminated politely with no contract between them and some platitude about not giving up, other agents had other priorities. Rachael was just about to choose that option when Rita stole her line,

"I'm the very last sort of client you need on your books. One who already has a full time job running a farm. And another raising twins. Who writes when she has time to shove a pen up her butt. And wiggle it."

"I wasn't going to put it in quite those words--"

"Had you done so, you would have been wrong. I never stick a pen up my butt. I'd have to take the broom out first. I've got no time for that."

The agent had giggled, as the first tiny cry of doubt in her unvoiced decision made itself heard.

"I tell you what. Here's Miss Muffet. And the first three chapters of Panic. There's more, but those pages are edited. And the outline. And a couple of soppy stories. I must go and move the sheep. When I get back, if you're gone. But they are still there. That's tough. If you can sell them, all contributions gratefully. 'N all that."

"Erm--"

"I've gotta go, Rachael. Catch the light!"

Rachael read the first chapter of Panic trying to assess it objectively. She was mildly annoyed to find it terminated half way through a public enquiry into the closure of the mobile antenatal clinic. The enquiry was a polite and legal, Twentieth Century re-enactment of Gunfight At The OK Corral. Rachael could hear the arguing Counsel, feel the fury of the villagers and taste the polish-laden air of the Council Committee room. The decision to close the clinic had been taken by the County Council, although they neither funded, nor administered it. The smell of sweaty fear pervaded her nostrils as Counsel for the Five Villages stood up to mow down the local politicians with verbal shrapnel.

As his devastating attack was about to begin --

She turned over to a blank page --

What the-- to her astonishment she realised that although she started out intending to appraise the work, she had **read** all three chapters. She had lived the experience of the young couple, coping on insufficient funds and struggling to scrape together on love alone a nest ready for a chick, only to be told,

"No it's chicks!"

The soppy stories likewise demanded that she read them from cover to cover, by which time the unvoiced decision had been revoked.

Rita had returned from herding the sheep up onto the fell, to find Rachael had left her a file, with a Post-it stuck to it.

Sign the contract and send it to me, and each chapter of Panic as soon as you can finish it. And all your soppy stories. We'll see what we can do.

Panic covered its advance and paid a steady trickle in royalties, and the soppy stories sold erratically for small sums. When Rachael rang her to tell her a well-known hirer out of drama scripts was interested in buying the rights to Miss Muffet however, Rita stepped in and vetoed it.

"No just sell a weeks performance rights. Direct to the Repertory Companies. Bargain basement price."

"They're worth more than that."

"I know about the Company you're referring to. They are exploitative, I won't deal with them. My Pantomimes were written for Kids. Schools, Youth clubs, Church socials. They are for Charity. Most of them. Let's not raid the charity pot just yet. While we've still got our noses above the slurry."

Reluctantly the young agent turned her thoughts to how she could turn Rita's generous charitable donation into one that carried Gift Aid.

"Okay. Have you thought about trying your novel yet?"

At the other end of the telephone, Rita glanced involuntarily at the locked chest and its searing scenes secreted within, some of which were coalescing into lengthy stories.

"Thinking, yes. There's not much to see yet."

"Extract the digit girl, it's the novel I want!"

"I know. I'll try."

When she put the receiver down, Rita apologised for the lie.

"Sorry Rae, there's loads to see, just hardly any I'm prepared to show you."

Chapter 31

May 1994

Sebastian

Sebastian's boss quietly resigned and left Toptofty and Sebastian found himself elevated to the Board into the vacant place.

This was it; he had arrived, decades before he could have expected it. He savoured the taste, like a good wine, and the fancy office and the generous salary.

But most of all he was savouring the perk that went with it, a PA. Moreover, she would be a PA that he could hire and fire himself, one that wouldn't scream if his hands wandered a bit. One that could be trained to expect the wandering hands, to welcome them even. Why his predecessor hadn't taken that route, rather than ham-fistedly, and repeatedly, attempt to prise Nonie Figgis out of her knickers, he'd never know.

Nonie Figgis of all people!

His PA would have nothing in common with her, he'd know her as soon as he saw her, there weren't that many about, but he'd know. No more jerking off in the toilet that overlooked the road on the off chance that something good was walking past.

Choose wisely, pay well and treat her correctly, and all the sex you could ever want Seb Stripe, will be there for the taking.

May 1994: Sebastian

He visited the local College and began the enrolment process in an Adult Literacy Course, choosing a time when the reception staff were run off their feet. He leisurely began to complete the form, then glanced at the queue behind him,

"I'll fill this out and get back to you."

"Yes. Right, next please."

He stepped back and, clutching his partially completed enrolment form before him like a season ticket, slipped through into the College proper. The room timetable guided him helpfully on his way. Business and Economics had a few girls, but not his girl, not the submissive, grateful mouse he was looking for. The next room a couple of students were trying to work, whilst maintenance was going on all around them. Further on, another typing class was full and gainfully busy, he was able to view the students inside without drawing attention to himself.

He saw her almost immediately, typing fast, never looking anywhere but at her script. Long, straight, dull-mousey hair cut in an unflattering style framed her downright plain face. Her complexion however was unexpectedly fresh and clear. Her lumpy, all-concealing blue top, clashed sombrely with the shapeless brown skirt of nondescript length. When the teacher approached, she barely managed not to cower. His barked commands were hurriedly obeyed, yet Sebastian could see that the barks were un-necessary, she had everything he required to hand. During the brief encounter he avoided touching her, unlike some other students who got touched, caressed and, in one case, fondled.

He wondered if she was called Maud too.

She was exactly what he was looking for.

The prowling Sales Director lay in wait until the end of the session then followed the students to their common room. The mousey girl hurried about her chores, being spoken to when required by the others, giving little smiles for answers, but obviously treating no-one as her special friend. The crush thinned quickly and Sebastian took his chance and approached her direct,

"I can't help but notice how organised you are. I was going to put this job advert up in here," he waved at the Vacancies board: "but I'll give it to you direct. I need a PA and you are exactly the girl I require. Had you just read the advert would you have applied?"

She didn't answer.

"I thought not, come to the works, for interview, on Saturday afternoon at two-o-clock. Security will be expecting you and let you in when you show them this sheet." He placed the job advert into her hand and waited, the girl glanced at the sheet then back at him. He pointed to his name on the sheet: "You say. Yes, Mr. Stripe."

"Oh. Sorry. Yes Mr. Stripe."

"And your name is?"

"Mary Andrew, Mr. Stripe."

"And a smile, Mary, to show that you are pleased, only you were chosen to be asked to an interview."

She smiled the little smile.

He nodded,

"We are a high quality textiles and clothing firm. We make clothes for high street labels, top end of the market. As part of the interview I will ask you to wear some of the company's products, my PA has to dress well. What size are you, a ten?"

"Yes Mr Stripe."

"Good. Two-o-clock Saturday? Bring any certificates with you. I know there will be others you haven't got yet." He tipped his head and waited.

"Yes Mr. Stripe."

Sebastian called in to see his Aunt,

"I think I've found somebody."

"Someone who will hold still to be tied up?"

"I think so."

"Make sure you don't hurt her."

Seb looked at her, surprised,

"Did I ever hurt you? I mean apart from--"

"No. Not in any way that I didn't want you to, but I'm family, special."

"If she's what I think she is, I'll take very good care of her. There is one thing though, she needs a makeover, can you?"

"Of course."

"Her name is Mary Andrew and she will really challenge your professional skills. I'm not looking for a princess, but there's a seriously lovely toad hiding deep in there, just waiting to blossom."

Confidently the Sales Director rushed off home, his mind full of lewd pictures of compliant, Mary Andrew eagerly acquiescing to being debauched. Her screams of pleasure echoed in his head as the orgasms raged through her bound body. Not immediately of course, but eventually, he could see it all. He filed away the half completed application form, supremely confident that he wouldn't need it as cover again.

On Saturday, he watched Mary being processed at the gate of Toptofty Textiles by Security and her faltering steps towards the entrance, obeying the pointing of the guards and his own directions on the sheet. She was wearing a cheap, brown, hand-me-down suit, which exaggerated the dullness in her hair and blue shoes. He walked over to the home gymnasium erected in the corner of his large office and made final checks, he nodded satisfied, everything was in place, although he probably wouldn't get to bind her to it today.

A few minutes later, but nicely on time, she tapped on the open door and sidled apologetically into the room. He could smell shower-gel and hair conditioner.

"This is no good," he barked: "I knew we needed to change your clothes, I didn't expect to give you deportment lessons too. Stand up straight, shoulders back, chest out, arms straight at your sides, thumbs down the seam of your skirt." Mary sprang to attention, watching him fearfully as he walked around her, examining her. "Posture better, keep it like that. But these clothes." He shook his head sadly: "I take it that is your best suit, for interview?"

"Yes Mr. Stripe." The worry came across in her voice; she obviously believed she'd already blown it.

"The job is to be a Personal Assistant. Personal! You will rarely be out of my sight; I need you to look good. Assistant! We will touch each other often during the day, so you have to feel good." He stuck an arm out: "Feel. Feel the texture of that cloth."

She obeyed him.

"The firm makes quality garments for the couturier market, so only expensive, stylish, fashionable clothes are good enough for the Sales Director's PA. You will be obedient, compliant and acquiescent and I will love you and cherish you in return. You tried to look nice for me, but you failed, no matter, I will teach you."

The abject fear in her eyes hardly paled at all.

"But it will require total obedience, compliance and acquiescence from you. I took the trouble to dress nicely for you today, did I succeed?"

"Yes Mr. Stripe."

"What do I smell of?"

"I think it's deodorant, you don't smell."

"But you should. You should smell of subtle expensive perfume, just the merest hint, as you walk past. Thorough bathing with shower-gel and hair conditioner, followed by deodorant under your arms and your fanny, is fine. They're a good start, they show you are clean and presentable, but you should smell too. Just a dot in your cleavage." He drew his hand down, seductively caressing between her breasts. "And behind each ear." He teasingly caressed right round them lifting the hair away and playing with her lobes. The fright in her eyes decreased as they dulled. "That shows that you have taken the extra step to think ahead." He waited teasing her neck with feather-light touches of his fingertips, his palms cupping her chin, while he looked enquiringly into her eyes. They focussed, brightening,

"Yes Mr. Stripe." He nodded and slid his hands down her shoulders and arms,

"Right, to business, these clothes. Take them off, I'm not going to interview you dressed like a lurcher's lunch, put a blouse and skirt on, over there, blouse and skirt." He sat at his desk and pretended to work. At first, Mary looked around, there was nowhere obvious to hide away while she changed, after a few moments she disrobed with her back to him and put the shear blouse and mini-skirt on, when she turned round he was looking at her, she blushed. “Much better, don’t you think?”

“Erm-”

“Don’t erm girl! Erm is vocal slouching. Say what you need to say politely and clearly and everyone will understand.”

“The blouse -- I can see through it.”

“Of course you can, so can I, you’re meant to, you have a lovely figure, you need to be loved for it, so don’t hide it behind a wall, drape it lovingly in silk.” He knew there was more; he forced her to say it with an enquiring look.

“The skirt; it’s very short.”

“No it isn’t. It’s the length a young girl with dreadful legs would wear. That is why I provided it, in case. Now that I can see how stunningly beautiful your legs actually are, I have decided that you will never wear a skirt longer than that one, and most of them will be shorter.” He could see he was getting through, instead of fear; there was now shocked acceptance in her eyes. “Your legs and bottom are your best features, even better than your lovely body, you will flaunt them for me and be loved and cherished, admired, appreciated and enjoyed in return -- Well?”

“Yes Mr. Stripe.”

“Even so, it’s still unsatisfactory, but with a few tweaks.” He walked around her pulling the clothes into place tucking, smoothing, arranging. A couple of times his dusting hand brushed over her bottom and her breasts. He handed her the company tie, then took it back again. “No. You’ll tie it wrong. Watch.” He drew her aside towards a mirror, turned her away from him, facing the mirror and draped the tie round her neck, sawing it back and forth to work it up under her collar. “Don’t slouch,” he reminded her as he pressed up to her back and began to tie the tie in a Windsor knot. “Twice round, but opposite ways, makes a neat triangular knot, remember, opposite ways.” His hands were frequently brushing across her breasts, as his erection pressed against her bottom. Her nipples thrusting out hard against his erratically brushing hands betrayed her emotions but, obediently, she neither slouched, nor made any attempt to pull away. “There that’s better.” He pointedly waited, looking at her through the mirror, head cocked to one side, whilst gently caressing her upper arms. After a moment,

“Oh. Thank you Mr Stripe.”

“Good, now let’s look at you.” He patrolled around her again, smoothing the clothes sensuously over her figure. “You’ll do clothed for the office, but that’s only the start. We aim for the top end of the market and my PA has to be a good clotheshorse too. You will frequently be called upon to wear the company’s products and we will often be away on business trips, sometimes at short notice -- Pack a bag we leave tonight, sort of notice, will your boyfriend object?”

“No. I haven’t got one.”

“Good, keep it that way. Then you will be able to do your job properly. Be a proper PA. Think of me as your boyfriend, I will need boyfriend type, intimate, personal services occasionally anyway, but you already knew that, because the salary on offer is far above that for a normal secretary.” He could see the shock in her eyes and hit it again: “You will make an excellent PA and be loved and cherished, by me and the clients you take care of. I expect you to anticipate my needs and fulfil them before I have to ask. I require complete obedience and instant compliance with requirements.” He watched the shock slowly be replaced by acquiescence and cocked his head again.

“Yes Mr. Stripe.”

“Good. Show me your certificates.”

The girl’s qualifications were very good, but Sebastian wasn’t really interested. The qualities he required, she had already demonstrated. He browsed them taking sporadic note. “Yes these will do. Your second interview is next Saturday, same time, same place. I will be assessing how you will look to clients, so between now and then visit Fanciful Fashions, speak to Maud. Get yourself properly measured and take delivery of a suit, a cocktail dress and casual clothes for travelling. Take notice of what she tells you about colour schemes, cut and style. Most important will be your lingerie. You need sensible cotton lingerie for travelling, but for clients you need something different. You cannot feel excitingly sexy if you are not wearing excitingly sexy underwear and if you don't feel it, you won't look it." Again he waited.

"Yes Mr. Stripe."

"Good." He produced a fat roll of notes: "Here's some money, for the clothes and perfume, buy something really nice, subtle, discrete and erotic. Expensive. With perfume, you only get the best if you pay for it. Find one you like and buy a small bottle, if I like it too, I'll let you buy a big one. Choose a well known, high-class Perfume House, one with a reputation to defend, there's less chance of being ripped off."

"Yes Mr. Stripe."

"And get your hair done, somewhere Maud recommends, not cut, just trimmed, styled, something simple, Pocahontas bunches or something. I want you to keep growing it long, something I can get a hold of, when required. Talk to the hairdresser about hair care, this time next week I want it shining with health."

"Yes Mr Stripe."

"Wear the cotton undies and the travelling outfit when you come next Saturday, have you got some good cases?"

"No Mr. Stripe."

"Then get some. A quality set of luggage that won't fall apart if a baggage handler drops his trolley on it. Maud will advise you. Bring all the clothes with you, to model them for me, neatly packed as if we were going abroad. Two-o-clock next Saturday."

"Yes Mr Stripe."

"Bring me the receipts. I'm not checking up on you, monitoring how much you spent, they're for tax. You're deductible, partly anyway."

Chapter 32

May 1994

Mary

Maud was really nice to Mary,

"You have a peaches and cream complexion, don't mess it up with too much makeup. Just the lightest dusting with this, to keep a shine off. This lipstick will make the colour in your cheeks stand out even more and match this eye shadow perfectly."

"I've not used eye shadow."

"Been told not to?"

"My Gran."

"They do that, I had a Dad like that. Now clothes colour schemes. Brown and blue don't lie well together, not usually. I would suggest that you avoid brown anyway. Pale pastel shades on top, dark skirts. Wear them short, you've got stunning legs, flaunt them."

"What colour should my shoes be?"

"Black, navy blue, red. Depends what you're wearing, but not mid blue, it's a non-colour usually."

"Not white either."

To Mary's surprise her mentor disagreed,

"Oh yes! But for games, specifically to play the tart. And you should have a pair of fuck-me boots too, secreted in your wardrobe, for the same reason."

Mary smiled the little smile.

"With long dresses, flaunt the tits. Go for a heavily tailored fit, tight in at the waist. You've got plenty up top, if you're going to cover up your best bit, your legs, bust the top out, they're nearly as good anyway."

"I hide them."

"Not any more girl, in future they have to see you coming minutes before you arrive."

"They're ugly."

"No they're not, they're lovely. Bust them out. I have some ideas ready to give you." Maud passed a file over: "And I made an appointment for you at ClipArtistes. You have good thick hair, it only needs a little TLC to become really nice. What do you think of the clothes ideas?"

"They're lovely, where do I get some?"

"Upstairs in the boutique. Was there anything else?"

"Cases."

"Ah yes." Maud plucked up another leaflet. "These are good, you get them upstairs too."

* * *

He'd touched her last week, it was only to straighten clothes and dust her off, but it had been really nice.

He'd been forgiving of the frump, surely he'd be involving of the attractive PA. Involving enough to step in and physically guide her. At home, before leaving for the interview, she studied herself in her mirror and tweaked until in her own eyes she was perfect. She then carefully placed some subtle errors. He would find them, of that she was sure, and he would just have to correct them.

Mary saw Sebastian watching again as she was processed at the gate. Her trepidation had gone, to be replaced by shy assurance. This time she walked straight over to the entrance and a few minutes later knocked quietly on his door.

"Come in, park the case by that desk and let me look at you." The girl obeyed him, then moved into the centre of the room and stood smartly erect looking at him. There was a gentle budding confidence about her, she knew she looked good. If the man she already thought of as her boss also thought she looked good, he would -- He would -- She hadn't thought that through, like 'lived happily ever after,' but she was in no doubt it would include touching. It had to. She'd ensured that it had to.

He walked slowly around her appraising her,

"Much better," he murmured, while confidently letting his hands do the 'looking', easing creases, smoothing wrinkles both real and imaginary, easing out every one of her errors. "Your hair looks lovely," he caressed it and slid his hands under it and released it. It fell back, shining and heavy: "And it will look better and better if you take care of it."

Mary stood still and quietly let him gently grope her while praising her appearance, the clothes and her ability to wear them. She was in such a high state of touchy-feelie pleasure that she nearly missed his next question.

"Yes you'll do. What's the perfume?"

"Trepidation Quattro, by D'Lintz."

"I like it, you may wear it whenever you want. Show me the clothes." He surveyed them critically. "Hmm. Maud chose these for you?"

"Yes Mr Stripe."

"You may model them for me then, they presumably look better on you, than in your case." He waited, making no attempt not to watch while the girl, again, vainly glanced round the room for somewhere to change and pre-empted her question just before she spoke.

"Come on girl, we haven't all day, if you get this job we'll be sharing a hotel room in Paris in a couple of months, frantically jumping in and out of clothes to make deadlines with clients, we won't have time to hide ourselves from each other then, get used to it now. Take those clothes off and put a new set on." Jerky and embarrassed, Mary turned her back and obeyed him.

"The underwear as well?"

"Of course, I told you why."

By the time she had the cocktail dress on, the girl's skin was pink all over. Sebastian stepped forward and smoothed the fabric over her body. Once again his touch steadied and calmed her.

"You do suit it. You look absolutely gorgeous; I should have known Maud would get it right. How do you feel? Like a sexy, complete-woman?"

The blush had largely cooled,

"A bit, yes."

"And so you should, because that is what you are. What do you think is wrong with your breasts, but right with your bottom?"

"I don't understand."

"You hid your breasts from me but showed me your bottom. Are your breasts ugly, different sizes, blemish ridden or what?" The raging shame caused a catch in her voice,

"They're ugly."

"Take the clothes off." Again, Mary turned her back and stripped. "Now turn round." She froze. "Stand up straight, arms at your sides and turn round. Every girl I've ever met is worried about her tits. Too big, too small, too high, too low. Ugly, misshapen, wrong. And every one of them is mistaken. You are no exception. Turn round. Don't slouch, head up."

There was a moment's pause, then she straightened up to attention and slowly turned to face him, the blush raging across her skin as she did so.

"As I thought, they're not ugly, they're beautiful."

Caught completely abeam, she spoke instantly and truthfully,

"My nipples are grey."

"Your nipples are large, and perfectly round, and the clearest, cool grey any girl could wish for, they are beautiful. Whatever gave you the impression they weren't?"

"My brother's friends spied on me in the shower."

"And they said they were ugly?"

"Yes."

"Did they spy once, or more than once?" Her head went right down in shame. "Head up! You're not playing the slave girl. Not yet."

She snapped to attention.

"Answer me!"

"Last summer. I didn't know. I live with my Gran, but I went to stay with my parents last summer. I didn't know you could see in through the shower vent from the garage roof. They spied on me every day, then when we came back to school, a friend told me."

"Do you know what they were doing when they were spying on you?"

"Laughing at my ugly tits."

"No. That's what they said, street cred and all that. Really, they were wanking over you, jerking off and spraying their spunk everywhere. Everywhere but where they wanted to spray it that is. Every single one of them wanted to spurt on your tits and that was only for starters. Why do you think they watched for so long? Believe me, Mary you don't watch something repeatedly because it's ugly, but because it's beautiful."

He stepped towards her and cradled a breast in each hand. Shocked, her eyes opened wide.

"These are beautiful. Big, perfectly round, smooth, unblemished-globes of beauty."

Shock was smoothly replaced by excitement. Just for a moment she thought of Mary Richards tied to her tree, with lust filled Indians approaching her. He continued holding her breasts until her eyes relaxed in acceptance.

"You must be proud of them and not think you ever need to hide them. You have nothing to be ashamed of. Now model the rest of the outfits without hiding."

By the end of the session she was standing before him stark naked and completely comfortable.

“Good. Third interview next week. I will show you our portfolio and examine you for obedience. My PA must be my strong right arm, but most of all obedient. I must know that instructions will be carried out to the letter, no matter what they are. Do you understand?”

“Yes Mr Stripe.”

“Good. You may get dressed now. Same time, same place next Saturday.”

Chapter 33

May 1994

Sebastian

When Mary arrived the following Saturday it was obvious that she expected to be admitted. She presented her credentials to Security, waited politely to be processed and then again, shyly confident, walked to the main entrance. Sebastian waited for her beside the open office door and began issuing his instructions even before she was in the room.

"Sit on the stool at the desk over there and look at the portfolio, sit still, do not speak unless spoken to, look right through it and examine the clothes, I will look at it over your shoulder and caress your body, while you read it, then I will ask you questions when you have finished." Mary hesitated only long enough to get her bearings, before she sat down and opened the book. It was a sequence of illustrations of formal gowns tracing civilisation, almost from the sketches on cave walls, through to the present day, a high-class couturier catalogue of the last seven thousand years. Sebastian pulled a chair over and sat cuddled up tightly behind her, his rampant erection pressed hard into her back. Gently, teasingly, he played intensely with her shoulders, running his hands through her heavy shining hair, caressing her neck and ears through China and Egypt, India and Italy, picking up her vibes noticeably. Had she been a cat, she would have been purring.

Occasionally she would reach out and gently caress the picture of a particular garment.

When she turned to the page with the Minoan décolleté gowns however, he slid his hands down to her waist and straight back up her front to fondle her breasts. He felt her shock, excitement and then her pleasure, as her arms lifted to allow easier access and her traitorous body relaxed under his caresses.

"You could be required to wear gowns similar to these at small discrete dinner parties. For me. For a few special clients. And to provide special intimate services for me, and very occasionally, special clients. Do you understand?"

"Yes Mr. Stripe." It was several minutes later that she reached out and turned the page.

Until she reached the end of the book he fondled her body sensuously, her breasts, her shoulders, her ears, everywhere he could reach. She sat quietly, with the book closed in front of her, a contented cat, gently purring, waiting.

"Do you understand completely?" He continued as if there had been no pause. "It's no use if you think providing intimate personal services just means washing my hair in the shower in the morning. It means way beyond that. Do you understand completely?"

"Yes Mr Stripe."

"Let's find out if you really do. You will be the person whose clothes you wear. Business suit, Businesswoman, Pharaoh headdress, a Royal Princess, there is a slave girl outfit in that box, take off all your clothes and put it on. When you are wearing it, you will **be** a slave girl." Again, Mary only hesitated long enough to identify the box, before walking over to it and opening it up. She lifted out the simple, white shift and its vibrant emerald green, limp rope belt, arranged it ready, then stripped naked before putting it on. Despite the apparent aplomb, she was pink again. Although clean and sweet smelling, the dress was designer-ripped and torn in places. She tied the soft rope around her waist.

"Walk over here." Her breasts were falling out of the front and the crooked hem occasionally failed to reach her thighs, but she stood still, straight but with bowed head, while he examined her and checked to make sure her body was completely available. "What do you think of the dress?"

"It is lovely material. It's very evocative, it's lovely."

"Yes, it is." He gently fondled her breasts and her bottom, the mild blush paled as, once again, Mary began to purr: "And you feel lovely through it. Good! Now then, imagine the slave girl has been captured by pirates. You've been in their hands for a week. They all wanted to ravish you and there has been no-one to stop them, just imagine it." His gentle caresses became more charged with purpose. "You have been ravished again and again, in every way possible, for a whole week."

Her eyes clouded, dulled.

"Oh, oh," she breathed, tiny sounds that were only just audible. He drew her over to his home gymnasium and hauled her hands up to the top bar.

"This frame is on the middle of the deck, everyone can see. The slave girl is handcuffed to this bar, she can't get free." Her hands grasped the bar firmly. "The pirates are going to sell you at the market tomorrow, so today they are all going to have their last go with you. Do you understand?" The bowed head nodded,

"Yes Mr Stripe."

"Good. There is just one more thing. When she was captured, the slave girl was terrified of what her fate might be; now she is sad. Why do you think she might be sad? Answer me clearly, there isn't a right or wrong answer, only obedience and compliance."

Mary didn't hesitate,

"She is sad because she is not going to be gang raped again. By sweaty pirates, debauching her body. After this last time. What has happened to her was not my fault, I had to do it, I was made to do it."

"You have discovered that you like the naughty-nice humiliation, you have been looking forward, all night, to being gang raped again. You are being made to do it, it is not your fault and you cannot be blamed for it. You fully understand, don't you?"

The bowed head nodded, again,

"Yes Mr Stripe."

"I'm just going to ravish you a little bit, not fuck you, not today. We'll do that in Paris. It will be nice to have our first time in Paris, won't it."

"Yes Mr Stripe," said Mary, with the little smile.

Sebastian stripped off his clothes and cuddled up to his new PA. He lifted her dress up and snuggled his rampant erection between her bottom cheeks and shagged against her, holding her hard to him with one hand across her chest, gently mauling a breast, while masturbating her with the other. Mary held onto the bar, readjusting her bare feet as necessary to facilitate his pleasure and consequently her own. It didn't take long, suddenly she screamed. Bravely she tried to hold the bar, but she couldn't and flopped. He had to hold her tight, to prevent her from falling as he energetically spurted up her back.

A little while later, in the shower, he explained what he wanted her to do and how to do it for maximum pleasure.

"And while you're doing me, play with yourself with your other hand. Make yourself come."

"Yes Mr Stripe. I will fall down when I come, I always do."

"Okay. When you need to, just fall down, I'll do what's necessary, but don't stop pleasuring yourself, until I say you can stop."

"Yes Mr Stripe." She knelt before him, rhythmically pumping him and sucking, while masturbating herself with her other hand. When she collapsed jerking and moaning, before he had finished, he followed her down and fed himself to her again. Obediently she swallowed most of his seed.

Later still, dried and dressed for the office, he surveyed his new PA and presented her with another thick wad of notes.

"Get yourself to a family planning clinic and get fixed up. Until I tell you different, I want you completely unable to conceive, I want you able to take on an army of Cossacks for a solid month and know you won't get pregnant."

"Yes Mr Stripe."

"Now your exams finish at the end of this month and there is a show in Paris a few weeks later. I want you in Paris. I need you to start on the eighth."

"Yes Mr Stripe."

"Have you got a passport? There's Denver and a long trip to the Far East later this year. We will be going to all of them, you will need visas too."

"Yes Mr Stripe."

"Every day you come in, bring me an item from your wardrobe. I will tell you whether you can keep it and when to wear it. Most of it we will throw out and replace with company items. Our PAs must look the part." He caressed her sensuously and kissed her tenderly. "How do you feel? Are you okay?"

"Yes Mr Stripe."

"Are you happy about your new job?"

Mary positively lit up from inside.

"Yes Mr Stripe."

"You are loved and cherished. There will be times when you will need to be disciplined, humiliated even, but you will always be loved and cherished, admired and appreciated. Do you understand?"

"Yes Mr Stripe. Thank you."

"That case is full of new clothes for you, take it with you, try the clothes on. Wear that skirt and the cotton blouses for college, with knee socks or tights and your own bra and knickers.

"Yes Mr Stripe."

"For work, wear the silk blouses and the short skirts. You can chose between knee socks, hold-ups, or stockings and suspender belt, change them about, randomly, surprise me, but no tights, not for work. If ever you're not sure, talk to Maud, she'll keep you right. There are some leaflets with lingerie styles, buy a selection of matching sets from the Exotic Range, black, red, you can buy a few white sets too if you like. On afternoons when we have no appointments, you may take your bra off. I may possibly even let you wear your blouse unbuttoned; and if you've been very good, I'll let you take your knickers off too and you can pretend that the slave girl is being examined for obedience, before being auctioned off. Would you like that?"

"Oh yes, Thank you Mr. Stripe."

"Chin up, shoulders back, chest out, you are the Sales Director's PA, you are **somebody**, look the part. The eighth, nine-o-clock on the dot."

"Yes Mr Stripe. Thank you, thank you so much."

He dismissed her with a smile and a wave of his hand.

Chapter 34

May 1994 -- December 1995

Mary

A shrinking and plain, quiet frump had gone for interview just two weeks earlier; although still quiet and unobtrusive, an attractive and elegant Company PA served out her remaining time at College.

The change went un-noticed by no-one.

Typical exchanges included:

"Wow look at those legs, they go right up to her bum!"

Mary surveyed the loudmouthed bully with cool aplomb and took him off at the knees,

"And at the other end, they reach the ground." She replied with the little smile.

And:

"Mary, are you doing anything tonight?"

"Yes, I'm doing something every night."

And:

"So what are you doing when you leave?"

"I've got a job."

"Oh, something nice?"

"Personal Assistant, there may be some travelling involved, yes nice."

"Oh. Who to? Where? What Company?" Was answered with the little smile and,

"Got to go, I'll be late, bye."

The lovely storybook had been read again since her first interview for Toptofty. Now that she actually knew, first hand, what a full blown sexual encounter felt like, Mary realised that the story needed updating, after all it had been written when women didn't have the vote, never mind the right. She didn't dare commit anything to permanent record while living at her Gran's house, but she spent the time profitably, her imagination unleashed, while she looked for and found a solution.

The day after her first salary cheque cleared, she moved into a rented flat. It was tiny, two rooms and a minute kitchen. She shared an entrance hall, toilet and bathroom with four other tenants. All five thankfully respected the rights of the other four to acceptable standards,

"Any spillages or dirt and you clean it up. There and then, no leaving it until later."

"That's fair."

"And we do the same."

Mary smiled the little smile and signed the contract.

Despite never having supervised such an event before, the new PA got all their bags, samples and presentation material to its destination in Paris, without a blot. Sebastian was also satisfied with the room that she booked. It was a small two-room suite, situated on the quiet side of the hotel, not too high, although high enough for a view. The reception room contained a seating area and a table, the bathroom positioned off the bedroom was fully equipped, up to and including fountain bidet and the bed was a four poster. While Sebastian fussed over his presentation address, Mary busied herself with chores, unpacking their cases, tiding away and arranging their dressing cases side by side in the bathroom. Presently there was nothing left to do and it was nearly dinnertime.

"What will I be wearing tonight, Mr Stripe?" Sebastian looked up. Through the sheer blouse Mary's breasts could sometimes be seen clearly when the light caught them just right; her proudly erect nipples betrayed how she felt about displaying herself. That they both knew she had nothing on beneath the skirt either, merely added to the spice of the occasion.

"Oh, what you've got on will do for dinner, later you will play the slave girl again, but really tied down this time, face down, on the bed."

She nodded and gave him the little smile, then sorted out the slave girl's shift and withdrew a small towel from a drawer.

"What's that?"

She showed him,

"Just for spillages -- in case -- I've never -- I've heard there may be spillages -- the first time."

"Ah yes, you will be lying over a pillow, Turn the duvet right down, put your towel on top of a pillow in the middle of the bed."

"Yes Mr Stripe."

* * *

Whilst kneeling up on the bed, Mary watched him intently over her shoulder, as he fastened first her left ankle to a bedpost, then the right. Then she arranged the pillow into a comfortable position and doubled the towel over it. When she was satisfied, she hoisted the slave girl's shift up round her shoulders and lay down. She reached out for the headboard posts, by the time Sebastian was organised to secure her hands, they were in position ready for him. He put clove hitches around her wrists and secured the ends in a reef knot around the respective posts, thus ensuring that although the bonds were not tight, neither could she get free.

"Are you comfortable? You could be there a long time."

"Yes Mr Stripe." He produced a pierced ball gag,

"This is to stifle your screams, it reduces the noise but still lets you breathe through your mouth as well as your nose." She opened her mouth and he nestled it in, buckling the strap behind her head. "Is it comfortable, can you breathe through it?" She nodded. "Try a scream."

She did so.

"Excellent, you can really let go when the pirates get busy beating and debauching you. Shall we begin?" She nodded and snuggled down closing her eyes.

"Right slave," Sebastian snarled in her ear: "We are selling you tomorrow, so tonight we will --"

She never opened her eyes again that night. Not even when he spanked her, firmly enough to make her grunt through the gag, not even when he deflowered her in mid orgasm, making her scream and jerk wildly; her eyes stayed closed, her face, between screams, in peaceful repose.

He climbed off her, untied the reef knots and retrieved the pillow from under her. She curled up like a child and settled for sleep with the clove hitches still in place. There had been spillages, but they had all been caught. When he unbuckled the gag, he took her hand and put her thumb to her mouth, obediently she suckled it. He tossed the duvet over her and snuggled in behind her, reaching around and gently pummelling her breasts through the thin shift. Only minutes later they fell asleep in mid pummel.

In the morning Sebastian awoke with a raging erection. His usual response to this frequent event was to masturbate. Then, Mary stirred,

"Are you awake?"

"Sort of."

He pushed her over onto her tummy, mounted her and fucked her energetically. The orgasms built and broke over her repeatedly. As he spent into her, she stifled her screams with her pillow.

The presentation was a success. A number of firm orders were finalised by contract, several more looked secure for a few days time. Sebastian spent some time with an elderly Frenchman negotiating the largest order. Mary sat over to one side watching the proceedings. With few exceptions the PAs fluttering about were young, ornamental, and well endowed. Several of them were male, but most of those were paired off with battle-cruiser sales women, although at least two had male bosses. Mary guessed that most of the sales executives and their PAs had the same relationship as she had had with her boss the previous night. The very few older auxiliary staff around were in turn accompanied by a young nubile assistant, who didn't seem to do much, presumably saving herself for later, with or without clove hitches.

The LeGrand contract required some serious haggling, judging by the time Sebastian was devoting to it, but eventually agreement seemed to have been reached.

Afterwards he briefed Mary.

"Tonight we are entertaining M. LeGrand in our room. You will wear the Minoan gown, the black one. No underwear. No. On second thoughts, wear the scarlet lace panties. Only the panties, not the bra of course. After dinner excuse yourself, retire to the bedroom and prepare the slave girl to be debauched. I'll leave everything ready, you should manage to get three ropes done up. I'll do your right arm when I come in."

"Yes Mr. Stripe."

"There'll be a blindfold this time too."

"Yes Mr. Stripe."

"Leave the panties on one leg, where I can see them and make sure you're comfortable, you could be there a long time. I want you wriggling about because the slave girl's getting her buzz from being gang raped, not because Mary Andrew's got cramp, understood?"

"Yes Mr. Stripe."

So M. LeGrand rated special client status, and with his shiny, swarthy skin, she had no difficulty imagining him in the guise of a sweaty pirate.

The slave girl is really going to enjoy herself tonight.

Quite soon, Mary was able to put down a deposit on a larger self-contained flat in a desirable residential area.

She moved in for Christmas and began the re-write of Mary Richards' Wild West Adventures.

Chapter 35

October 1995

Roger

Presently, Roger became aware that his cuddly dolly, had replaced her voluptuous nubile pneumatics, with a hard core of muscle.

"What do you think you're doing?"

"Taking up my career again, Roger. Slavishly drudging after you and your kids twenty-four hours a day was never part of the deal. Wife, yes. Mother, yes. Slave no."

"Get that liberated tabard off woman, and your knickers while you're about it!"

"Make me!"

Roger grabbed her and made her. Half an hour later, satiated, she glided back down out of orbit, wriggled out from underneath him and went for a shower.

"And there'll be no more mention of taking up your Police Career again."

"No dear."

Once showered and dressed, she paused at the bedroom door,

"I'm off, I'll pick the kids up on my way back, you'll probably have gone to work, see you tomorrow."

October 1995: Roger

"Where're you going?"

"I told you. Bye."

"I said, no more mention of taking up your Police Career!"

"And I said, 'no dear'."

Despite his precipitous evacuation from the bed and furious calls after her, his wife merely waved as she departed.

Her intentions became clear to her parents over tea at their house.

"What do you think you're doing?"

"That's exactly what Roger said. I'm taking care of me and my brood, Dad. I never deceived myself that Roger was for the duration, hoped yes, believed no. So I'm getting myself qualified for when the pigeons return."

Chapter 36

October 1995

Rachael

Rachael rang Rita and set up their meeting, in Rachael's annual tour round her clients.

Over coffee the agent gently chided her author about the lack of any sign of the promised Novel by Poppy.

"I'm sorry."

"I know that farming and twins won't leave much spare time for dedicated writing but--"

"It's not that. I'll come clean. I can write five thousand words a week. Week in, week out. But you couldn't sell them."

"I need an explanation."

"Explicit sex."

"Ah, the old sex and violence bit."

"No, just sex. I hate violence. Rachael, there's something you need to know. I have a criminal record. For two years I worked as a child prostitute. My early teens."

The other neither baulked nor blinked, merely glanced at the window, through which Colin could be seen working. "It's okay, Colin knows. He picked me out of the gutter one night. I've not fucked anyone else since."

Despite her visible best efforts to stem them, the difference for the better in her life during the last six years got to Rita and she filled up. As the tears flowed, Rachael jumped up, pulled her chair across beside the distraught girl and cuddled her in.

"He's been so good to me. Given me love, a home, two lovely kids. Don't get me wrong, I'm grateful. But the only thing I want. He cannot give me. Sorry. I haven't bubbled like this since I came home after my first night on the game."

Rachael waited until Rita was back in control before she released her,

"You okay?"

"Yeah. Sorry."

"No problem, can I ask? What is it Colin can't give you?"

"Me. He can't give me, me. I'm Poppy the ex working girl. Poppy the Author. Rita, the Mum of James and Jane. Colin's wife. Common law wife anyway. But I'm not **me**. I don't know who **I** am."

Incensed, the agent attacked the concept vehemently,

"**I** know who you are, I walked in here that first day we met in May and knew you intimately."

Rita narrowed her eyes.

"I had deliberately and with cynical calculation arrived two days early. Specifically to see you unprepared. When you catch people with their knickers down, you're more likely to see the real person, rather than the facade. I walked into a house that had a happy, contented soul. The rough draft of the Parish Magazine was lying there on your desk, half edited. There was fresh tea in the pot and homemade cake on the table. In the lobby a large, fit and healthy border-collie bitch was nursing a litter of pups in a stout, open-sided kennel, while being watched over by her mate. The place was deeply clean and tidy and smelled of new baked bread, the latest two loaves of which were rising by the fire. You were in the middle of making a party dress for Jane and you had to leave me to move some sheep. I knew you instantly and intimately and liked what I knew."

Rita just sat quiet looking at her, the crisis had passed, but Rachael could see the emotional wall going back up,

"Just look around you, Rita, your me is the heart and soul of this place, just open your eyes."

As the futility of her protests became more and more obvious, Rachael shook her head and retreated to the safer topic,

"Anyway, that apart, I take it that you saw your fill of violence on the game?"

Rita too gratefully dropped the dangerous subject to concentrate on simpler matters,

"Oh yes. Just a time or hundred." She replenished the coffees. "But not sex. I love sex. I liked it when I sold it. I often got to come with a stag party." She sat back down. "The trouble is, all my heroines are me."

"No they're not!"

"They are. Different aspects of me. Camouflaged to make it less obvious. Mes that I feel comfortable with. But they all love sex and drag anyone into bed that doesn't say no. The poor sods don't even have to say yes. Look, I'll show you a couple. Fairly mild ones. I'll go and feed the chickens while you read them. Saves embarrassment. Then you'll understand."

Rachael had to agree with Rita, the enthusiastic mattress hopping of her heroines meant that most Women's magazines wouldn't touch them, whilst the lack of coercion or S&M ruled them out from most of the porn market too.

"But don't discard anything. When you're well known, if we give your readers warning, they may want to read your porn too. I do, I find it fascinating. Meanwhile keep trying the novel, someday something will trigger the flood and you'll have a best seller on your hands, trust me, I'm your agent. Mind; there is one searing, page-charring short story you could try and pull no punches doing it, that I'm sure I could sell. Write up your first night on the game, if you can, the Top-Shelf Mags would almost certainly be interested. And you never know, it might give you catharsis, even if only for that night."

Chapter 37

March 1996 -- May 1996

Roger

The Redcombe pigeons returned rather sooner than expected. A string of clandestine affairs surfaced, when Roger, again, carelessly impregnated a colleague. The girl was on secondment from another force as part of a long-term investigation. It turned out that her local politician husband, surprisingly, could count up and he reached only seven, when he should have got to nine, and kicked up a major stink.

The baby silently gazed at the new face presented to it,

"I know babies are not supposed to be able to focus," said the proud father: "But you would think she was. It's probably because she's premature, they are supposed to be more advanced aren't they?"

"So some people think. But your daughter isn't premature," said the nurse innocently. "She's full term, which means she'll be very bright I should think."

At home the local politician checked his appointments diary closely and then that of his wife.

He thought it through and then carefully picked his time, a couple of months later, when the proud grandparents had taken their granddaughter away for the day, to show her off to relatives.

"Who is her father?"

His wife stiffened, turned and looked steadily at him.

"Please don't lie to me, don't make me get her paternity tested. I never demanded you keep your legs closed and I know that I can live with a cuckoo, and love her like my own, but not so sure that I could live with a lie. We have never lied to each other, please, let's not start now. Is she John's?"

"He says not, he says he spent the night with Wendy, she says he did too. They say she's Roger's. We had a party, the night we got the breakthrough, cracked the alibi, Roger and I left together, so I'm told. I don't remember anything from about ten-o-clock onwards. Just, I didn't have any knickers on when I woke up. I didn't have much on at all. I'm not claiming I wouldn't have done it if I'd been conscious, but I wouldn't have done it unprotected. I wouldn't just wilfully risk foisting a cuckoo on you."

"Drunk, or date rape drug?"

"I drink even less away from you, than I do beside you."

"So that leaves rohypnol?"

"He will have had access -- Where do we go from here?"

"I love you, that hasn't changed. I never regarded infidelity as grounds for anything much. And the circumstances barely qualify for infidelity!"

"What if I'd done it willingly, without the rohypnol?"

"And why might you have done that?"

"He's beautiful, and sexy, and a dangerous bastard. Exactly the kind you fuck for the thrill, but don't marry, not if you've got any sense. What if I had?"

"It would be grounds for a good spanking, probably several good spankings."

"Well I didn't and that's the truth. But---I--there's a small chance that I would have done if he'd asked, does that get me the spanking?"

They looked steadily at each other, then she wriggled her skirt up, peeled her knickers down her thighs and half turned her bottom to him. When he reached out for her, she helped him lay her across his knee.

Roger's Inspector didn't like the telephone call that he received the following day. The Inspector checked, got his facts straight and Roger liked the resultant interview even less.

Leaking insidiously, as gossip told gossip, it wasn't long before the message reached the first jealous discarded-mistress. From then on it was only a question of time before the news was being gently cooed in Mrs Redcombe's ear. The whisperer was blissfully unaware that the imaginary embellishments with which she adorned the account were mere pale approximations to the truth.

The divorce settlement included an alimony agreement that Roger regarded as crippling, besides the swingeing child maintenance payments.

Chapter 38

June 1997

Colin

Colin had been up all night with a cow in labour. Rita joined him, a mug of tea in each hand.

"I've called the vet. You said I could. If there was no change by eight and I've done it."

"He'll not get paid again, not for months."

"Yes, he will. The post's been. Rachael's sold another of Poppy's short stories. And royalties from a couple of pantomimes. We'll give him that cheque. Keep our noses above the slurry. Best thing I ever did. Getting her as my agent."

"From where I'm looking she got the good deal, your stories sell themselves."

"Only because she knows whose nose to shove them under. But it does mean we can do it. Pay the vet."

"What about the tax?"

"Don't worry about it, the accountant says I'm still okay."

"I don't deserve you."

"I know you don't. But in the very pointed absence of anything better, you're stuck with me. Get used to it. The first 20 years are the worst."

June 1997: Colin

"What are we going to do?" He asked, grinning at his girl, in spite of everything.

"None of that. Save this cow. And whatever little treasure she's carrying. Take it one day at a time from there. Here's the vet."

"When did you call him?"

"After eight. It's always after eight, somewhere."

The vet had gone, after helping to increase significantly their new tiny herd of quality beef cattle by two. Rita continued the conversation he had interrupted.

"We're getting there. Every year, we're that little bit better off."

"When do we break even?"

"We're getting there."

"When?"

"In our lifetime. The twins won't inherit debt. And I might write my novel. Rachel says she'll sell it no problem. I just need to think of a storyline."

"One where the heroine doesn't go bed-hopping across half the County?"

"Something like that."

Colin smiled and gave his girl a hug, but later, alone in the bathroom, the mask fell away, a prematurely old man looked at him from the mirror.

"Our lifetime? No, Rita, yours possibly, the twins probably, but not in mine, I'm on a countdown. Five years tops, I'll not see our kids married. I'll not see us married, never mind the twins." The telephone rang and a minute later Rita's call came up the stairs.

"Colin. There's another plonker out on the Moss. On a Trials bike."

"How long has he been missing?"

"Since yesterday lunchtime. Everybody thought he was with somebody else."

"I'll take the quad."

"Okay. They're meeting at the rescue hut in half an hour."

"Okay."

Chapter 39

July 1997 - August 1998

Mary

Mary Andrew's business trips, many domestic, but some foreign, several times a year, fell into a predictable pattern. The first night away she would always have sex with her boss, with, or occasionally without being spanked, or tied up, or both. On other nights, she would usually be subjected to a longer multi-partner sex session, always tied, gagged and blindfolded. Mary would imagine the slave girl, captured Princess, helpless business-woman hostage, whichever costume she had been instructed to wear, being gang raped, being forced to submit and therefore blameless, and be sent off on a roller-coaster orgasm lasting hours.

Each morning she would examine herself surreptitiously for damage, but to her surprise, she never found anything worse than interesting and occasionally exciting bruises. Within a few days, not even they could be found and she occasionally had to resort to mild disobedience to get them replaced.

The reality was that Sebastian filtered her clients. He had no intention of risking any harm happening to his own private Personal-Wet-Dream-Fantasy, any clients he even suspected would be rough with her did not get through the door.

The outcome was that Toptofty Textiles, despite being at the expensive end of the market, held its own during some rocky months of trading.

Nevertheless, the fluctuating fortunes of others, confirmed that the rocks were close and jagged.

Mary, sniffing the financial air like a suspicious deer, caught the fleeting nuance.

She was delivering a portfolio to a prospective customer, but when she arrived at the Novochester Talon-vert, the hotel receptionist told her that Madame Petite was out but had left a message for her to wait. She withdrew into a corner near the lifts and was just about to sit down to wait, when a salesman from one of Toptofty's most aggressive competitors walked into the foyer. Mary slid behind a Monstera deliciosa, which was trying, with some success, to take over the entire corner. The salesman reported to reception and was directed to a chair.

Mary admired the deeply divided leaves she was hiding behind. Someone who knew about Cheese plants had collected the aerial roots, directing them into large clumps of damp moss fixed to a massive supporting stake. That explained the plants vigour. She suspected that a different hand had inserted the label, which read Philodendron pertusum. The salesman stood up, crossed towards her and entered a lift that was being held for him by someone inside. As the door closed she saw the pair greet each other. She doubted that it was a lovers tryst; the warm handshake she had witnessed was professional, not personal. If anything however, that was even more worrying, the girl was a fellow PA, she knew her well. The girl's boss would not be far away.

For the next hour, Mary fretted anxiously, imprisoned in the hotel foyer, but as soon as Madame Petite returned and she had delivered the portfolio, she returned to her boss to express her doubts. Ironically, they were in a company whose representatives did not partake of the pleasures of her body,

"That Uncle Sam Clothing Company, they are looking towards other suppliers."

“Sam’s my oldest customer and my best, he knows when he’s on to a good thing.”

“He’s looking, Mr Stripe. Do not put your trust in princes, they let you down. I’m being a loyal PA, warning you.”

“Yes you are my lovely and you deserve to be rewarded. Go and prepare yourself, when you come back, have no underwear on.”

Mary closed the door and locked it,

“I already did that.”

When the possibility of her compliance being a factor in the securing of the contracts crossed her mind, Mary resolutely crushed it out, replacing the thought with a picture of her bosses face, repeatedly telling her she was loved and cherished. She coped with her menstrual cycle clashing with other commitments, by taking the pills continuously for the odd weekend. Then one of the extended trips to the Far East heaving itself up over the horizon included the whole five days. She checked this time.

“-- so will you need the personal services?”

“It depends little sugar-bunny. I’ll do you in the shower quite happily, but you only entertain clients if they’ve signed the contract. Never before, only if and after! So we’ll have to see.”

“Yes Mr. Stripe.” With her usual serene face, but the demons were out of the box. Now she had to face it. She was Toptofty’s Top Tart. She was the carrot, the girl who paid for completed contracts, by spreading her legs!

“And take care of yourself, quite a few of the machinists are off. Some sort of flu or something. I don’t need a sick PA who’s not going to Australia.”

“Yes Mr. Stripe.”

With five days to go Mary set her watch back nine hours and changed her eat and sleep pattern. By the time the departure day arrived, she was thoroughly Jet-Preed. The Jet-Lag would balance her up nicely on arrival.

Chapter 40

July 1998

Roger

The cleaner was unlocking the door of the reprographics room.

Brilliant, thought Roger, he could collect his work without having to trek through to the office, No need to grovel to that ugly and officious Office Manager for a key.

The rotund little cleaner scurried about, emptying the waste-bins and shredder hoppers into her capacious bag. She grumbled mildly because she had to pick several screwed up papers from off the floor. Roger kept out of her way, preferring not to test whether he could play skittle to her bowling ball.

"I hate this you know. Them leaving papers on the floor, it's bad enough when they're screwed up, you know it's rubbish, but when it's not, is it rubbish or not?" She was appealing to him and indicating printed papers that had slid off the table.

"It'll be rubbish -- No it's not, it's the Newsletter, the rest are, like, up here, they go on this pile here."

The first item on the Newsletters lying on the side bench caught his eye, grabbed his attention and forced it to the page.

It was a notice congratulating a young fast track promotion seeker on securing the job as boss of the new training complex, and the elevation to the rank of inspector, that went with it. Roger took no further notice of the bustling cleaner; he didn't even hear her parting,

"Goodbye, shut the door when you leave."

The top letter slowly crinkled and crumpled as he screwed it up in fury.

Police Sergeant Roger Redcombe hated a lot of things.

He hated the announcement in the letter. He was supposed to get that job, not the latest in a long list of graduate upstarts, some of which he'd trained.

He hated those who regularly flew past him on fast-track promotion.

Most of all he hated being an officer in the service.

He had enrolled as a copper in the force, and, when his superior's backs were turned, he still was, as several villains nursing old scars, as well as old scores, could testify.

He stuffed the rage-crumpled letter out of sight and searched for his work.

The bouncy, new, blonde secretary, all bust and bum, entered and greeted him politely, before heating one of the copiers and loading her work into the hopper. Roger had to concentrate on finding his work, to avoid meandering off into muses about what he would like to do to her. The copier heaved its long suffering sigh of readiness and the secretary printed one copy of the first sheet, to check the quality.

Yes, thought Roger, *I'd give you a night to--*

"Oh shit. What's that doing there? That's not mine."

Jerked out of his reverie at last, Roger saw she was looking aghast at the paper that the copier had spewed out. He walked over. It was a copy of the alarm layout in a building, complete with Master Codes.

"I must have picked it up with my stuff by mistake. Look, there's more, it's a whole file."

Obediently, Roger looked,

"Shred the copy. There should only, like, be one and return the file. Work out where you got it from and return it quickly. Now!"

"Yes, I'll do that."

Roger headed out of the room with his work.

"See ya," he called. "Bye."

He opened the door, checked that she couldn't see him, shut it and slid quietly behind an adjacent cabinet.

The nubile secretary hurried past and scuttled off down the corridor, holding the file tightly in both hands and batting it from side to side to counterweight her strides.

Roger collected his bonus from the shredder hopper, shredded a couple of Newsletters as misdirection, then he too left the room, and only seconds later, the building.

At home, in his cold little flat, with the door locked and the curtains drawn, he removed from his pocket thirty or so strips of paper. The plan was shredded slightly on the cross he noticed with pleasure, that would make re-assembly easy.

By the time he took a break, he had rebuilt the photocopy perfectly and the plan of what to do with it, was already forming in his mind.

If the authorities wouldn't pay him his proper dues, here was a chance to take them.

Fencing the stolen goodies would be easy. There was a prestigious building in a European capital city, where, unchallenged, he could walk in the door carrying jewellery on fire. A few minutes later, he could leave with a banker's draft that he could cash at any building in the World sporting the words Bureau de Change.

Getting the hot gems from their alarmed cabinet to the capital city was the problem.

It would need a lot of planning and not a little luck.

As an extra level of security, the alarm layout bore no indication which building it referred to; moreover, he could not read it. Even if he was standing in front of the correct Alarm Box, open, there was nothing he could do about it, the symbols on the diagram meant nothing to him.

The following day Roger bought a 50,000 map of the area and the 25,000 sheet that covered the bit of Bollyfaith Moss in which he was interested. He studied them minutely.

There was only one road to the Museum. Five whole miles of it, it was a certain trap, if anything went wrong; so certain, that although he would use it to gain access, he would not return along it, even if things went right.

He visited the place and noted the valuables that he wanted. Not the priceless historic artefacts that he would have difficulty placing, he concentrated on the less famous, second league gems, those that could be easily reset, or even sold on as found. With three accomplices, he could still get away with several million pounds worth in the safe timeframe he'd worked out. A stroll through the Museum gardens confirmed what he had suspected from viewing the maps. The Museum stood on a promontory overlooking the Snake River. A fit and healthy man could scree jump down the slope into the river, but couldn't get back without making a serious detour. Moreover, the nearest road was half a mile away, in the forest, and that was assuming that he could find a way through the barriers without anyone becoming suspicious. The only route out was the opposite way, the impossibly dangerous one, across the Moss.

He needed an electronics expert, an exporter and a guide.

He needed unknowns, who consequently would not be suspected, who he could control and manipulate, and he had a candidate for each slot. Moreover, they all needed some quick money.

It had taken a while to set it all up, but as autumn approached, he was ready.

Chapter 41

July 1998 -- September 1998

Ben

The selection board of Bentwistle Electronics were reviewing the performance of the applicants in their respective interviews. None of them was what they really wanted, but it had been decided to keep the appointment in house and of a moderate lot, Ben had come out best.

"He's a button sorter."

"They're all button sorters, just he's the best one."

The discussion rumbled on, but eventually it was decided to offer Ben the job, as a sideways move, rather than a promotion.

"It's not the job I applied for."

"It's what ever you make of it, Ben."

"And not the money."

"It's half the money down and the rest in five increments. Show you're up to it and the rest is available, even in a timescale shorter than annual, if you merit them."

Ben was able to swallow his annoyed pride, while it was coated with the honey of the raise, even if it was only half what he had hoped for.

The erratically brilliant youngster who was promoted to act up into Ben's now vacant chair, promptly solved the problem that had been holding up the design of the new chip by the simple expedient of removing an array. He called a meeting of his technicians,

"I want to test a new chip circuit. Make the front end the same as the latest version, but set it up without the second library array."

"You'll have no error trapping for when an operator calls -- Oh, I see what you mean."

"With the modifications elsewhere, they're redundant, those operator calls now become null calls."

The new design, no longer waiting for irrelevant replies to inappropriate calls, worked first time. Such a simple answer to the problem, predictably produced grumbles from subordinates, who hadn't spotted the solution themselves.

"Why didn't we do that before? It's obvious when you think about it."

"Blinkers and pride. He suggested it to Ben weeks ago. But it was Ben's array. It was a vital improvement last year, when it was new."

The new chip with its vastly enhanced features, was faster, cheaper to produce, on a smaller die and consequently used less power than the one it replaced. Most important of all, it was a pin for pin compatible swap out for the old one. Circuit boards already in production could support it, without retooling. All over the World, Purchasing Executives read Bentwistle's flyer extolling the merits of the new chip and reached for their telephones.

* * *

The Management Staff Meeting was, unusually, garnished with canapés and wine,

"Well done everyone, we got there." Old man Bentwistle surveyed the assembled crew of white-collar workers with obvious pleasure. "The first orders for the new chip are already coming in. Today, a tipper-truck, tomorrow, an avalanche." Ben turned away, bile setting his throat on fire. It was always the same, you got headhunted by a different department and the one you leave makes the breakthrough.

"Never mind, you could always leave us next week," said his new section head: "Then it'll be our turn." Had she genuinely been able to read his mind, she probably wouldn't have turned her back.

As soon as he could, Ben telephoned Megan,

"Put some gnomes out. Six!" and hung up.

There were five stupid little garden gnomes disporting themselves about in front of the carport when he got home.

He drove his 4x4 over them repeatedly, but if anything that just made his humour even blacker, his wife came out to the front, as the coloured plaster joined older splodges nailed in all over the drive.

"There were only five."

"I said six!"

"I'm sorry, there were only five." Ben leapt from the cab, leaving Megan to switch the vehicle off after it had parked itself against the back wall of the carport. A row of smashed bricks at bumper height showing that it wasn't for the first time. He stormed through the house looking for the cat, but Tootles had decamped the moment she saw the gnomes being put out.

Chapter 42

August 1998 -- September 1998

Mary

There were two typists pressed into service in reception. The flu epidemic had not just decimated the works; administration was now creaking under the strain.

"Morning, Mary, you're still vertical I see, but looking a bit peaky."

Mary returned the girl's greeting and explained,

"The peaky bit is because I'm working on Australian time, it's late afternoon for me. I had a flu jab back in May, best thing I ever did, judging by the wreckage all around the works. I had a bit of a snuffle last week, but medically I'm fine."

"Your boss isn't, you have to go yourself." She presented a horrified Mary with a new file of instructions from the Board.

"He has to be fit! We're supposed to be on the afternoon flight. It's not just Australia; it's the Asian Tigers as well. It's twenty days, five presentations. I need him."

"You're going alone, best of luck," said one typist: "I'm glad they promoted me only as far as the front desk."

"And me! Bring me back a Koala," finished the other.

The wisdom of going to meet the time shift, days early, was borne out when Mary disembarked from her thirty hour flight at eight-o-clock in the morning local time, refreshed from sleep, and ready for breakfast. Several times she dressed herself in a full outfit she was to wear at the presentations and rehearsed in her hotel room psyching herself up each time, like a good actress before going on stage. The result was a string of polished performances, a number of orders and contracts signed and an eager rabble of wide boys on the make. A typical encounter would begin,

"Right, Mary, you know how it is, dig out the handcuffs, make it worth my while and I'll give you a big order."

"You give me the big order, and when it's signed, I might be accommodating," she replied: "But there will be no handcuffs." And walked away.

He got the same blank wall treatment the following day too.

"But, Mary, I need to get confirmation for an order this big, I'll get it but--"

"Then get it. Sign the contract and then we'll see. You're in Britain next month; give me a call. If the deal is done, we'll see." By the end of her trip, her appointments diary had a number of names, dates and places pencilled into a list.

Parting with samples had released space in the company trunk for presents. There would be more available after Korea and Japan, meanwhile, Mary went looking for Koalas. Although the big retail stores all stocked them, she searched until she found a smaller business, which specialised in soft toys. At noon the middle-aged manager took over, while his small staff went to lunch. Mary entered seconds later.

"Yes Miss, can I help you?"

"I want a couple of Koalas please. One for me and one for a friend." Several sizes and styles were examined and gently cooed over, and Mary settled on her choice.

"Those two are really nice ones Miss. Twenty for that one and fifteen for the smaller one, that will be thirty-five dollars please."

"I was hoping for discount for two?"

"I can go five percent for the pair."

"Have you got a back room, or stock room where we could negotiate for a few minutes?"

"Er -- Well--"

"You'd better lock up, through here is it?" said Mary already on her way. She stopped when he didn't move: "Go on. Lock up. I'm going to give you a much nicer time than you can buy for thirty-five dollars anywhere in Australia. And I'm going to do it twice, today and tomorrow, once for each bear. You don't want anyone walking in on us and spoiling it for you. Do you?"

On autopilot the manager walked over and locked the door, Mary nodded, took his hand, and led him through to the stock rooms in the back.

"You can do whatever you like, wherever you like and however you like. Just if you want to do me standing up, be ready to catch me, I fall down when I come. I came dressed ready, there's nothing under the dress, just me, come and feel."

To the managers astonishment, the following day she returned, again at lunchtime, to pay for the second bear. He had thought the promise to be empty, and although he had been perfectly satisfied to settle for one instalment, enthusiastically helped her fulfil the agreed deal.

* * *

A visit to work would take Mary hardly out of her way home from the airport and she called in, as much to keep herself awake as anything. The typing pool was busy, with empty seats, it was obviously still recovering from the epidemic, although the girl Mary wanted was there. She crossed over to her and plonked the Koala on her desk.

"I presume you didn't want one that eats shoots and leaves?" she said. The other girl laughed.

"No. Thanks, it's lovely. How much?"

"Nothing. I fucked him for it. But you owe me." The girl looked startled for a moment, then burst out laughing, along with her friends. Mary nodded and left for the Directors suite.

Lazarus Long was right, she mused, One of the most convincing ways to lie, is to tell the absolute truth.

She arrived at her office and replaced her relief, just in time to pick up the telephone, place the call on hold, and walk through to announce it personally,

"Uncle Sam on line two for you." Sebastian, still looking pale, smiled weakly at his PA fresh back from the Pacific Rim; he hadn't known she'd arrived.

"When customers call you to ask for their contracts to be renewed, it prepares the ground for them to receive the bad news about the new price. When did you get back?"

"In time to answer the telephone." She waved at the outdoor clothes that she was still wearing.

"Ask him to hold, put him through in two minutes."

"It's the boss, Sam himself."

"Two minutes, Mary, not a second less, and then lock the outer door and come through. I need some of your tender loving care, that flu bug was a killer." When the telephone rang he picked it up and launched into his spiel,

"Hello, Sam. Sorry to keep you waiting, but we've got so many orders for our new line. Filling them is going to be a real problem--"

"Hi Seb," interjected Sam into the momentary pause: "I'm sure glad to hear that. I called to tell you personally that we've signed up a new supplier, we won't be needing any more from you. I didn't want you to hear it from someone else, I'm glad it seems to be easing problems for you -- Seb -- Seb --"

In the outer office, Mary locked her door and prepared herself to lose a wrestle with her boss, discarding the items of clothing that could be ruined otherwise, but when she went through she found Sebastian white and staring, with the telephone receiver lying on the floor.

"I'm fired. Bound to be, I've lost that contract. I'm fired."

I warned you! Leaped to Mary's mind, but she said nothing. She also said nothing about the contracts that could be signed in hotel bedrooms from Betws-y-Coed to Berwick upon Tweed, if she was cooperative enough over the next few weeks.

If it's my body that's buying the deals, perhaps the time has come to cut myself a bigger slice of pie. So, when she reported back the details of the trip, it was only the polite interest shown and the straight up front contracts, that were included. Not the promises that Mary knew exactly how to turn into signatures, that were secreted in her other briefcase. If Sebastian really had blown it, his replacement was already sizing up his shoes.

Chapter 43

September 1998 -- October 1998

Roger

Roger crept up on the Business Fraud Specialist, who was sitting alone in the canteen, intentionally from behind.

"Just the man I, like, want to see."

"It'll cost you, there's a stag night coming up."

"Supply only. You pay her fee, all I want is, like, a nod or shake."

"What?"

"Toptofty Textiles. I've, like, got the chance of some shares, yes or no?"

"Can you get that new girl, Robyn?"

"Yes."

"The shares are available because the rumour is they've just lost their biggest customer, so what do you think?"

"Keep my hand on my ha'penny."

"You're sure you can get Robyn?"

"Yes."

"Go for Bentwistle Electronics, they've made a breakthrough in controllers. It's short term, buy now, sell in three or four months, before the Tigers reverse engineer the chip."

Roger hid his disappointment, if Bentwistle had a new chip, Ben was doing okay. It was still only two down, how to get at Ben? Through Megan? He'd intended to hold that in reserve, Ben was a vengeful git, more likely to go for revenge than cooperation.

He sporadically watched the Brown house, whilst trying to work out a strategy, and witnessed the murder of the gnomes and the angry exchange that went with it.

The following day he called on Megan,

"I was in the area with time to kill and wondered if an old friend could, like, give tea, in exchange for solace?"

"Tea you can have, solace you may not give. I don't need any." Roger stepped up to the door. "And you're not coming in. Sit on the patio in full view."

"You'd think I was untrustworthy!"

"Quite wrong. I'd trust you to the gates of the hot place itself, but it's what I'd trust you to do, that you wouldn't like."

"Oh, Megan!"

"You stay out here, you get tea and chat only, take it or sling it."

Roger sat down grumpily,

"I take it. Heartbreaking way to treat an old friend."

Several minutes later Megan returned with the tea,

"I'd still love to give you solace." The hangdog look would have been comical and persuasive, on someone else.

"No way. I know that look, one inch given and the knickers are off. I need your solace like a dose, the depressions only temporary. I don't need your solace to make things permanently worse."

"What happened?"

"Ben changed departments, just before they got the breakthrough to the new chip. So the new job's not tasty-treat-time at the minute. But it will be, when he settles in." Roger relaxed, having sifted out the loyal wife's supporting slant and come up with a truer version. Ben would, at best, be feeling he was owed, that would do fine.

* * *

The car rolled to a halt at the kerb, none of the girls moved. The window slid down.

"Robyn."

"Shit!" But she said it softly. She walked over: "It can't be my turn, I only paid you at the weekend!"

"Keep Friday night free, you're, like, booked for the whole night, the usual 20% for me."

"You're a bastard." But she had sensibly waited until the car had left.

The following Saturday Roger sat himself on a bollard outside Ben's newsagent.

"Hello."

"Hello, Ben, I've been waiting for you." He began straightening off his paper, in preparation to folding it up.

"Megan said you had called, but that you had not been rude this time, I had wondered why."

"I didn't mean, like, to be rude last time." He only just remembered in time what he had said. "It was pique, that she'd chosen you over me, I admit it."

"So what do you want?"

"Your professional expertise, which your employers are ignoring so thoroughly. I want to hire your skills for one night, the pay's, like, very good."

Ben looked around, there was no-one near,

"But the work is illegal?"

Roger didn't reply, just continued folding his paper.

"Exactly what do you want?"

With Ben on board and Sebastian flapping about in shallow water looking for a net to surrender into, Roger turned his attention to the hardest target, but ironically, the easiest lever. He picked up the telephone and called in his biggest marker.

"Hello."

"Hi Jake, it's Roger."

"What do you want?"

"Just, like, an exchange of paper."

"How much?"

"No really, I just, like, want some paper." There was a long pause: "Headed paper, blank from vice."

"I can't."

"Just one headed blank from vice."

"I can't they're numbered."

"Sure you can. Take one out of the middle of a pile, knock coffee over the rest, they could, like, be in the shredder before your secretary's got her knickers back on."

"I want everything."

"I'll trade everything, photographs, negs, like, the lot. In the post first thing tomorrow, send it to the house not the station and I'll send your stuff."

The temptation to hold something back was very strong, but Roger thought it through again, then put all the incriminating photographs and their negatives in the envelope to trade. The last thing he needed when he retired, would be a resentful vice officer, looking for revenge.

* * *

Colin saw Roger cutting through the Market Day crowds to accost him.

"Hello."

"Hello, I've, like, been looking all over for you."

"Working."

"And me, like, on your behalf. Have you got a quiet pub in this outback, where we could talk?"

The back room of the Swan, was, as usual, deserted mid morning.

Colin declined a pint and Roger cut directly to the game,

"This came yesterday." He passed an envelope across. "I can smother it, but if I do, that's me done for, like, no further promotion, ever, I'll be a Sergeant in the sticks for the rest of my career."

Colin examined the paper inside and went pale.

"If I smother it, I want something big in return. You drive a robbery getaway car over Bollyfaith Moss."

"I can't."

"Yes you can, Colin, like, what you're saying is, you won't. I would have thought Poppy was worth it, never mind Rita."

The Sergeant didn't push it, just outlined plans that assumed that Colin was on board. When Roger asked would he provide the meeting place for the business proposition, the farmer reluctantly agreed.

"Come at ten-thirty on Thursday. Rita goes to town on Thursday."

Chapter 44

October 1998

The Meeting

On Thursday, Colin was mildly surprised to see that the members of the gang included Ben.

"Right, shall I start then?" Roger took silence for assent and walked over to the window: "Lovely view, Colin, nice farm, like, hard work, but a moderate living, enough to raise your kids. Thanks for providing a nice secluded meeting place for me, and you two, thanks for coming." He turned; the other three watched him in silence. "You have a nice job, Sebastian, but for how long? You have a good job too, Ben, in fact we all have, on the face of it, but the reality is different. We all have a serious problem. Hard work, no money. I would like to change all that, with your help. I'm offering you equal partnership in a job. One job, like, well paid. Are you interested?"

"Go on," said Ben.

"Colin's mortgaged to the hilt. Interest charges are crippling the farm. Sebastian loses his biggest customer at the end of the year and won't get him back, he's in serious soft and smelly. Your company has just ripped you off again, made millions out of an idea, gave you a few hundred as a thank you. We all need money. Like, my increment didn't cover this year's alimony increase."

"What? I mean --" Sebastian stuttered to a halt.

"I can provide a large payment for one night's risk-free work. It's, like, illegal of course, but everything is insured. It's unguarded, we can take what we want and be set up for life."

"What is it?" asked Sebastian, apparently regaining some control.

Roger looked around the room, "Bollyfaith House Museum."

Silence.

"The Big House a few of miles up the valley towards Low Trefoille houses art treasures of unimaginable value. And it is isolated, unguarded and, apart from, like, the state of the art security system, a sitting duck."

"What's the catch?" asked Ben.

"Who do we have to kill? Nobody. The catch is none of us can, like, do it alone. You will deal with the electronics and silence the alarm." He waved at the businessman: "Sebastian will export the treasures and Colin, --" He paused to smile at the farmer: "Colin will get us away over Bollyfaith Moss. It can't be the forest, the ravine between it and the house is, like, impassable. I will provide the know how. We are a team, every member vital, but in a different way."

Sebastian seemed horrified,

"We can't -- it's -- it's --" But his voice was frail and faltering.

Colin, still hoping for an out asked,

"Is this guy really here?" while looking at Ben.

"He's analysed the situation, so I suppose yes."

"None of us has a choice," continued Roger. "I get passed over for promotion in favour of college boys who know nowt, Colin's debts are killing him. Sebastian is in danger of being fired and you." He waved at Ben. "You are getting, like, ripped off. I'm offering a risk-free way to solve all our problems."

"There is always a risk," said Ben.

"Okay, like, I'm offering less risk than driving to work every day." There was a long silence.

"You're going to do it, aren't you?" Said Colin to Ben.

"Why not, I could drive into a tree on the way home. Sebastian?"

"I'm not losing my job, I've already lost it. They'll have me out, as soon as they see the figures."

"You wouldn't get half a mile across the Moss without me."

"Are we all, like, agreed, then?"

"How do I silence the alarm? It's not likely to be from down the market, it won't have Mickey's arms telling the time."

"What would you need?"

"Nothing less than the engineers access codes."

"These? Like, for example."

Ben studied the paper, the others crowded round him.

"These precisely! Like, precisely for example." Mimicked the engineer.

"Are we, like, all agreed, then?"

Roger leaned forward over the settee and placed his hand out flat, while glancing at, Ben, Sebastian covered it.

"One for all?"

"And all for one," said Ben, as he added his hand.

"I suppose so," murmured Colin, his hand reluctantly completing the stack.

"How do you know which building this is? There's no mention," murmured, Seb, voicing thoughts for all of them.

"There's no mention for security, if this paper was lost, like, fell into the wrong hands." He leered. "It would be valueless. But, I know which file it came from. They're the codes we need, I promise you."

"We're old lags if they're not," murmured Colin.

"I'll need to visit the place," said Ben after studying the re-assembled pieces of shredding again. "That's vital," waving at the paper: "We couldn't do it without, but I'll need to see the bits in situ."

"It's called casing the joint and, like, we all need to walk around it, even Colin, despite not going inside. Next week, all on different days, you all visit. Okay? Ben?"

"I'll go on Monday."

"Colin?"

Presently the meeting broke up.

Chapter 45

October 1998

Ben

As arranged, Ben paid the museum his visit the following Monday. Like Roger before him, he took note of the outside of the building as well as the inside. The steeply sloping site must have forced the builders into constructing a cellar; much of the allegedly ground floor was way above ground level. When Ben spied the short door in the wall below the kitchen, he gave himself full marks for predicting its existence. From its appearance it most probably was the original door, which could not be opened from the outside. Hinge bolt heads apart, it lacked furniture of any kind. He guessed from the well-worn track to the door that much of the food arrived into the kitchen through it.

Inside the museum the control box was in full view, trumpeting the fact that the building was protected. The keypad was at a comfortable height for a normal teen-aged girl. He looked away; he'd expected nothing less. What he really came for was elsewhere. Not upstairs, although he perused the jewellery that was the main target of the planned burglary, his real interest lay downstairs, among the Rembrandts, Rubens, Turners and Lautrecs. He found five that were suitably sized, they would do lunch nicely. Having achieved his primary objectives, he took tea in the café and gave himself further Brownie points when he saw a junior chef emerge from the cellar, through a trapdoor in the floor, carrying a side of pork.

That night he took the train to the coast and a taxi down through the docks to a quiet, secluded and dangerous, waterfront pub. He peered in through the window first, but then, satisfied, paid and dismissed the cab. Coolly, he walked inside; silence fell. He went straight up to the bar and ordered a mineral water, which he took to an isolated empty table. For several minutes he took sips from the drink. Presently a huge gorilla stood and began to make his way across towards him.

"It's all right, Frankie, he's family," said a man at the bar, without turning round and the gorilla resumed his seat. Ben sipped his drink, the bar, for the first time since he entered, was full of murmuring voices. Presently the man who had spoken into the hush, picked up two glasses and joined Ben.

"Hello, Ben, mineral water I believe." he murmured.

"Hello Matt, yes thanks."

"So what brings a long lost cousin hunting for black sheep?"

"A week on Friday, late Friday night, I will have five old masters, Rembrandt, Rubens and Turner. Each one is worth millions, but they will be extremely hot, which knocks their resale value, I know. I want half a million in a Swiss bank, the price is not negotiable, it's a cut rate to Family. I'm giving you first refusal."

"How long have I got?"

"Eight days to let me know if you're able to trade. Once you find a buyer, my guess is he'll not be able to sleep until he has them." He slid an envelope across: "These are the specs."

* * *

The call came through to Ben's desk, at work, a couple of days later,

"I've got a bad case of insomnia plaguing me for a cure, let me know as soon as you can help. Bye."

Chapter 46

Early November 1998

Sebastian

If there was one thing selling had taught Sebastian, it was to listen to the vibes. Failing to do so regarding Uncle Sam had been costly, so when the others at the meeting were transmitting that they had their own agendas, Sebastian had taken note. He didn't trust Roger to pay the shares. What if he was in charge, he could be trusted to share it out properly.

But how can you become in charge?

Dead easy, steal it in transit, you'll know exactly where it is and where it's going, it will be a trot up.

And if nobody realises it's you that stole it --

Despite crushing that thought instantly, it kept recurring.

He specifically engineered a slack time on Monday afternoon.

"Mary, I want you to do something for me."

She came in and locked his office door.

"No. If you're good we'll do that later."

"Oh. Alright, what is it?"

"Count Runtoli, would you find out his release date for me? He's in gaol, somewhere in the mountains, I think."

"That's what I thought too, but apparently not, he's out on pre-release licence, to integrate him back into the community. I'll call you as soon as I get him on the line."

Sebastian jotted down the headings he wanted to cover with the Italian, leaving space for notes. The Count was feeling the pinch even more than himself and possibly could do with a friend.

List for call to Count Runtoli: -

Jewellery to export. 11th November.

Must not be inspected by Customs. Hot!

Consignment worth at least fifty million sterling.

I can give details of transfer, but you will have to steal it.

~~Yours for ten million.~~ No!!

Ask for twenty settle for ten.

Mary traced the Count and put him through.

By the end of the call several sentences had been added to the existing notes.

List for call to Count Runtoli: -

Jewellery to export. 11th November.

He's Interested

Must not be inspected by Customs. Hot!

He can handle Continental end, but I must deal with British end, need to think about that!

Consignment worth at least fifty million sterling.

He can handle that.

I can give details of transfer, but you will have to steal it.

No problem.

~~Yours for ten million.~~ No!!

Ask for twenty, settle for ten.

Settled for ten!!!

What about Mary?

She'll want to give it all back.

Can't have that, she's had a good run.

I'll easily find another,

shouldn't be too hard, with ten million, or even a couple of million!

With that much I could have Nonie Figgis!!

Sebastian studied the notes for a few minutes, smiling with satisfaction, then put them down.

He patrolled his office thinking of ways of smuggling valuables past suspicious Customs officers. Thoughts that were constantly side-tracked by muses on what Nonie Figgis' price for being tied up might be. There was a tap on his door, he plucked the sheet of paper off his desk and fed it into the shredder before Mary, peeping in at him, had a chance to see it.

Chapter 47

Early November 1998

Mary

"Is it later yet?" she asked.

He picked up a hank of soft rope,

"Yes, I think so."

Smiling the little smile, she entered and locked the door behind her.

Afterwards she inspected the exciting new bruises spreading over her bottom.

"Will they keep you happy for a while?"

"Oh yes, Mr. Stripe."

"There's some collating to do, it's on my desk, and can I have a coffee please?"

"Yes Mr. Stripe."

"No on second thoughts, I haven't time, get me a Pepsi from the machine please."

"Yes Mr. Stripe."

"I'm going to my brother's birthday bash, I'll do these at home later."

Mary got dressed and carried the work out to her own desk.

Sebastian began sorting the papers he was going to take to work on at home. A title sheet was missing. He went through to Mary and swapped her the report for the can.

"Do me another front sheet for this please."

"Yes Mr. Stripe."

"It will be me, I know. It's most likely that I've gathered it in with other work. Who knows when I'll find it?"

Sebastian returned to finish packing his briefcase, while he quenched his thirst. Mary printed off another title page just in time to complete the report and for her boss to take the offered sheets as he breezed out past his PA.

"Goodnight Mr. Stripe."

"Goodnight, Mary."

Mary drew her soft cushion from its cupboard and sat on it carefully. Then reached for her work.

The top sheet began,

List for call to Count Runtoli: -

Jewellery to export. 11th November.

He's Interested

She read it through carefully, then thought for a minute.

She walked through to her boss' office and checked the shredder bin. She didn't even have to open it up. She could see through the transparent side of the hopper. It was sliced up and concertinaed, but the original of the title page she'd just printed, was still identifiable as the last sheet shredded.

Something on his desk caught her eye; it was a pamphlet. In glowing terms it urged the World and its Family to visit Bollyfaith House Museum and admire the treasures inside.

Back through in her own office she finished her work, whilst unsuccessfully trying to blot Nonie Figgis out of her mind.

* * *

Early November 1998: Mary

At home, whilst riding the little bear, she read about Mary Richards saving for the price of her ticket, her fight on the top of the coach and her subsequent adventures, living alongside and loving the man who had rescued her.

The version she read, however, was one that she had written, and enlarged, and developed, as she learned at the hands of her many lovers. Although it had as satisfactory and happy an end as the original, no open British publication could have printed her version at the start of the Twentieth Century; very few would have dared at the end of it.

Mary rode and fell off her little bear, again and again, but eventually, exhausted and sore, she had thought her future as PA to a cheating thief through and decided on her actions.

Chapter 48

Early November 1998

Police

"Kirkdale police, how can I help you?"

"There's going to be a robbery at a big house. Jewels. Antiques," said a thin breathy voice: "I'll ring with more details tomorrow. Tell Hattler. I'll need a number to ring him direct."

"What is your name, Miss?" but the line was dead.

Inspector Hattler, young, eager, inexperienced, but a tenacious thief-taker-in-the-making nevertheless, set the line up and made sure he was available to take the next call. The traces on the mobile led to

Ms G. O. Offy,
10 Neeland,
Paris,
France.

Hattler deciphered the code, with neither research nor a prompt from his Sergeant.

"That's a dead-end then, Mick."

"Yes Guv, I'll follow it through, to say we did, but you're right. Do you want the credit stopped, try to flush her out."

"No, let's keep communication going. See if the company can find a favourite transmission spot, but for the moment, let's assume she's genuine. Start thinking up some possible targets."

The favourite transmission spots soon proved to be supermarkets and shopping malls, anywhere where a mobile would be expected, rather than noticed, but strangely, from the wrong side of the Tyne gap.

Possible targets were legion and at the present state of knowledge, all equally likely, any preventive cover would have to be spread too thin.

The tip off, though, had been accepted. Three men were to raid a target in Cumbria on the night of Friday 11th November. When the call came through on the Friday, at the last minute, changing the target to the wilds of Northumberland, the logistical difficulties meant that Hattler had to hand over the operation to Northumbria's finest. They accepted the commission without demur and invited him to commute over aboard his chopper to be in at the kill.

"I don't understand, no quibble, just come over and join in the party."

"It's weird Guv. But we are going, aren't we?"

Chapter 49

Early November 1998

Rita

Although Rita knew nothing of the problem; that Colin was desperately worried was confirmed in early November when something happened that had not happened since she moved in.

Or more to the point, didn't happen.

The something didn't happen the following night either, nor the one after.

Rita collected Jess and set off to walk the forest boundary with the Border collie, armed with a small roll of wire, a bag of staples and a pair of sophisticated, heavy-duty fence-pliers. Some walkers, beaters and especially animal rights activists, were not always as caring of the fabric of the land as she would have liked. She had expected to find holes and she found one, by the Snake River. That meant she would have to search for errant sheep,

Never mind it'll be something different to worry about.

She could see one or two sheep up the valley, so she decided to go up through the forest to the Snake Bridge and work back down the little river rounding them up on her way. It meant a there and back walk of several miles, but as the forest provided little fodder compared to the river valley, that's where the errant sheep would be. The bridge also marked the limit of stray; beyond it the pickings were even more meagre than the forest. She called Jess to her, put her on a lead temporarily, climbed through the hole in the fence and dropped down the steep Vee shaped gorge, all the way down to the riverbed.

During the winter, the Snake River was occasionally a raging torrent, ten metres wide and half that deep. She could clearly see the Winter-Flood-Level tidemark of twigs and leaves trapped in branches on the opposite bank, several metres above her eye level. Now, in autumn, she could cross the entire width of the water with only two steps and keep her feet dry.

Once in the forest Rita released Jess again and let her quarter the firebreaks and forest roads to her hearts content. The collie flushed rabbits galore. Near the end of their trek, they passed Bollyfaith House Museum. Although the building was out of sight to the West, she knew where she was, because the rabbits were replaced by pheasants and grouse. There were always grouse, straying over from the Moss, where the forest encroached close to Bollyfaith House.

Ben drove his Landrover through the forest navigating his way to the Snake Bridge, not that he remembered its name. A worried Rita, on her way to round up absentee sheep, saw him briefly through a gap as he drove past. Later, Ben rode back on a bicycle. Again, Rita glimpsed him from the trees, but again he didn't look her way.

As they approached the Snake bridge, Jess ran on ahead eagerly to the minimalist concrete slab laid across from bank to bank and drove out the escapees from under it, but instead of returning, stood looking under the bridge. She turned to look at Rita and barked once. When Rita joined her and scrambled down to a level where she also could look under the bridge, she found Jess was attempting to flush what appeared to be the same Landrover Ben had been driving, parked out of sight. She couldn't even see it from a few yards away.

Then the other worry resurfaced and she forgot about Ben.

That night Rita rounded on Colin in their bedroom,

"Have you gone off me or something? You haven't touched me for three days."

"No, of course, I haven't."

"I never thought the day would come--"

He cuddled her in,

"Stop. I haven't gone off you, as you can feel. I'm horny for you all the time, it's just -- Com'ere. This is how much I've gone off you."

The squealing, jerking activity ceased, Colin climbed off his girl and panting, collapsed down beside her.

"Okay -- You haven't gone off me -- So what's the problem?"

There was a long silence, but they'd been here before.

"You're not going to sleep until you know, are you?"

She shook her head in the darkness,

"No."

"Do you want the plausible lie, which will allow us to live together, or the truth, which might have you packing your bags in a few minutes time." She looked steadily at him, her eyes flashing in the gloom.

"You're serious aren't you?"

"Yes."

"Is it another woman?"

"No."

"Man?" His stomach jerked with the laugh.

"It's not sex, it's robbery."

"Tell me. Tell all."

At the end of his narrative, she cuddled her man and held him close,

"You're not doing it."

"We need money, an --"

"We paid a thousand off our debt last year. This year it will be more."

"But w--"

"I'm selling more stories. You're not doing it."

"I--"

"I meant it to be a surprise. I won a prize, a short story prize. It paid the feed bill for six months. There'll be no crimes!"

"I want out but--"

"The man I love is not to drive that getaway truck. Poppy can go back on the streets bare arsed."

"No!"

"Well that's how strongly I feel too."

There was another long silence.

"I have to. I'm sorry but I have to."

The bed-head light went on.

"This isn't about money is it?"

Colin didn't answer.

"It's about me, they couldn't get to you through you, you're squeaky. They got to you through me!"

Again, he didn't answer.

"Well, if ever I was unsure about how much you loved me. I'm not now. Thank You. Tell me."

He shuffled uncomfortably,

"Just tell me darling. I need to know."

Her man heaved a deep sigh through his nose,

"There's been a Police File check, from a Company in London, on Poppy the Author. Roger'll doctor it if I drive, keep the info secret, stop Rachael finding out."

"There hasn't been a check, so he will not need to doctor it."

"There has, he showed it to me. An official letter from Vice in the Met. I've read it, it's code numbered and everything."

"It was a forgery. I know that for a fact. Because I'm on the Police National Computer. It's all there. My working name, my real name and current address. This address. Johann Beaks told me when he updated it. My conviction for soliciting, everything. And the fact that I'm going straight now. And, Rachael knows all about it. There's been no check, because there's no need. It's all available. To every Copper in the land." Colin closed his eyes and sighed deeply,

"Message received and understood. How do I get out?"

"I'll talk to a clam friend of mine. You can tell her everything. She'll think of the way out. There's something else too. You've reminded me."

Chapter 50

November 1998

Elaine

Elaine Jepson listened impassively to Colin's account.

"Could you really drive a truck over Bollyfaith Moss and get through alive?"

"I do it regular." He referred to Rita. "We both do, with the rescue team. We're always fishing walkers out and idiots on off-road bikes, sometimes we even get them out alive, but we never see the bikes again."

"Blood and Sand! Okay, here's what you do. You stay with it right up to --"

Rita dropped Elaine in the supermarket car park.

"Does, Colin know what I am?"

"No. Well I haven't told him."

"Okay, are you ready, it's got to look good."

"I know. Do it now. The right person's watching." Elaine took the younger girl's face in her hands and smooched her lips, tongue, everything.

"Wow! That should be good enough, did you kiss your female clients?"

"Not on the mouth. Not as a general rule. There was one special one. I can feel the watching eyes. Boring in. D'y'want another?"

"No, I liked it too much. You take care now, little Poppy."

"I will, I promise." Elaine decamped to her own car and Rita waved her off before leaving herself, whilst avoiding eye contact with Mrs. Guggenheim. It would be all over the district by suppertime.

'That tart up the Vertlea Farm, two timing him with a girl. I saw them kissing and carrying on.'

Rita giggled, by the third retelling she would have had Elaine spread naked across the bonnet, if that was all.

Colin could sail an ocean liner up High Trefoil village-street now and, provided she stood on the deck, no-one would notice.

Chapter 51

Friday 11 November 1998

The Museum

The Landrover crunched round in a wide arc to a halt at the side door of the museum, facing back the way they had come.

"Okay, Colin, Two Beeps you leave the lookout--"

"And come running. I know." The men got out. Colin adjusted his yellow woolly hat and then headed off back down the road, while Roger stuck his wrecking bar into the frame and heaved, the frame collapsed taking the door with it. Ben loped over it and trotted through to the security box, already bleeping its response to its slumber being disturbed and calmly typed in the lengthy engineers bypass code. The box fell silent. He set to work removing the cover.

"What are you doing?"

"My job, double-checking that there's no sticky strangers inside, quietly dialling up the local nick. No it's okay, get your jewels, I'll finish up here." Roger and Sebastian hurried off up the stairs, past paintings and statues worth millions, but too big to carry. Ben identified the simple capacitance and resistor-pair timing-device, and turned the pot down to half its value, before replacing the cover. He retrieved a lightweight folding rucksack from beneath his jacket, slipped into the study and out again with five small old Masters, stowing them in the ruck as he headed for the kitchen.

He dropped down through the service trap door,

and sprinted along between racks of stores,

to the short door.

He laid the rucksack down beside it,

and threw the heavy bolts to the outside.

Then he called Hattler, in the breathy voice,

"Change of plan, it's Bollyfaith House Museum. Hurry they're there now," as he ran back up the gangway, to join the others.

The robbers made two trips with jewellery and returned for some paintings.

Ben's personal alarm began vibrating sensuously in his pocket.

He let the other two get ahead of him up the stairs,

stopped behind the statue of Nelson on the half landing below the second floor,

took a firm hold of the statue,

and waited.

All the furies opened up,

as the tampered-with timer kicked in,

and triggered the alarms.

Ben heaved his lordship through the landing window with a loud cry,

then slid behind Lady Hamilton.

Nelson hit the ground in the quadrangle below.

Roger and Sebastian came gunning down the stairs.

"He's gone out of the window."

"Serves him right, the plonker. Electronics expert! Like, no!"

The robbers cleared the stairwell at a dead run,

and fled to the side door.

Ben followed silently,

but heading for the trap door,

he dropped through and closed it behind him,

and dashed to the short door,

grabbed the ruck,

and ran outside.

Roger and Sebastian raced for the Landrover.

The chunky figure of the lookout was lumbering towards them across the car park, Colin's yellow woolly hat pale in the starlight.

"Hurry! That bloody Ben's killed himself."

"Like, falling out of a window."

They dived in the rear doors.

The shambling runner grunted a reply,

reached out for the door handle,

and the police pounced.

Lights blazed at them from all sides.

"Armed Police. Freeze."

Shadows jumped out, Police wielding handcuffs.

The back door of the Landrover was yanked open.

Inside a uniformed policeman was struggling with a suspect.

The cuffs went on as those outside watched.

"Take him away," said Sergeant Redcombe.

"Well done Sergeant, very well done."

The proffered hand was accepted,

and another pair of handcuffs snacked smoothly into place.

"But not quite well enough. Roger Redcombe, I arrest you --"

Rita sat on the brow of the hill, anxiously watching the circus below her in the Museum car park. All the activity was concentrated around the Landrover. There was no interest beyond the circle of lights. She spoke continuously, describing the scene while Poppy's dictation recorder whirred softly in her lap.

Ben skated ankle deep in pebbles down the scree into the ravine, crossed the Snake River and ran up the shallower slope on the other side. At the top, he turned and looked back. The outline of the building rose up above him starkly black against the aura from the brightly lit car park, as noisy as a disco, on the other side of the building. A helicopter was descending into the blaze, while all around him, was calm and quiet darkness.

"I'd expected a greater time lapse than that," he murmured, his soft words carrying a relieved sigh. "But it's perfect! That's for the saddle, Boris's Bum Boy, sneering at people while pretending to help and all the other slights and hurts -- and especially for fucking my wife before I got to have her."

He smiled to himself, then turned and trotted up a firebreak to the forest track and turned heading for the Snake road.

When he reached the decrepit road, he paused and looked back again, Bollyfaith House Museum was half a mile and a hilltop away, neither light nor sound disturbed the dim scene before him.

He moved down to the bridge and dropped down into the deep-pit-blackness under it.

He slung the ruck in the rear of the Landrover,
felt his way along the side,
opened the door and got in.
Tipping his head back,
he breathed deeply.
After a few seconds rest,
he retrieved the ignition key from its hiding place,
thrust it into the ignition,
and switched on.
Nothing happened,
no lights,
no sound,
nothing.

There was a firm bump on the door of the Landrover, which rocked the vehicle slightly and then a floodlight came on, revealing a beautiful blonde standing beside it, holding a warrant for inspection.

"Ben Brown, I am Detective Inspector Elaine Jepson, and I'm arresting you--"

Ben flung the door open to smash her face, but smashed his elbow instead, DI Jepson, had chocked his door shut with a pit prop braced against the underside of the bridge.

"--on suspicion of--" continued the police officer to the end of her statement with totally unfazed aplomb. Then she turned to her uniformed minders: "Nick him," she said.

Chapter 52

Friday 11 November 1998

Finale

Mary Andrew re-read her letter of application for the job Director of Sales, which she was pretty sure would become vacant as soon as Sebastian sold his stolen jewels. When she secreted it in the briefcase alongside the confirmed big orders that she intended to use as her credentials collateral, she was totally unaware of the imminent tornado which would bounce her into a Sixth Months Trial in the Toptofty Boardroom sixty hours later.

Megan Brown settled down to watch her favourite video while Ben worked late. The telephone rang, and when she answered it, the caller blew her World apart.

Constable Redcombe drove the police van round in a circle ready to drive straight out when she'd picked up her cargo of villains. She jumped out, walked round the back and opened up. She had to help a shocked and shaking Sebastian climb unsteadily into the truck. She turned to supervise the second prisoner in and came face to face with her ex.

"Oh no," she said sadly. "This was always my worst fear."

Friday 11 November 1998: Finale

Rita watched the activity in the car park changing focus. People had been loaded into a police van and removed and attention switched back to the Landrover that Elaine had provided. It was being thoroughly examined. Rita could see the flashes as photographs were taken. Nearby a silent shadow moved.

"Your coat's here. Put it on before you cool down. And your hat. Don't catch a chill."

"That copper that took my place is a big boy, he couldn't fasten the other one, had to hold it closed."

The rotors on the helicopter began to move.

"Oh! They're going, time we were too. Just in case the infrared camera's on. And that pilot's a bit keen." The couple picked their way across the Moss to their quad, fired it up and Colin drove them home.

"Did they get him, do you think?"

"Elaine will have got him. I've known her since before she got married. She used to be in vice. Sees two kinds of crime. Those of necessity, of need. And those of wickedness and greed. Where wickedness is concerned, she's a heat seeking missile. He can run. But --"

"I'm glad you stopped me."

"It's Megan I feel sorry for. I bet she waits for him. To get out. And he won't appreciate it."

"I feel guilty."

"You were lied to. To call a spade a bloody shovel. You were blackmailed into agreeing. Then you were betrayed. Double crossed."

"I know."

"Would they still have tried it? Without you?"

"Yes, most probably."

"Then you probably saved their lives. Roger and Seb anyway." Rita waved at a letter propped up on her desk. "And something else. Cast your bread --"

Colin opened the letter. He turned goldfishing, his trembling hands barely able to hold the cheque for many thousands more than their overdraft.

"Rachael's sold Poppy's story. The full pornographic, bed-hopping version too. Just on the synopsis. To a film company. That's just the option. Like a first refusal payment. To stop me selling to anyone else. There'll be much more. If they take the option up."

"What story?"

"The great Bollyfaith House Museum Scam. If you ask me again I'll say yes this time. Now I've got something decent to offer you. Now I can be an equal partner. Now that I know who I really am."

"-- Rita R-R-Roundheels," spluttered Colin in a whirlwind of hope, expectation and despair. "Will you marry me?"

Rita -- Who?
The End

If you liked this novel, you may be interested in these other books by Petra Ceason.

Janie, Mechanic On A Motorbike

{Due to be released 2015}

Janie Jones is the youngest of a family of two girls and a boy; she is small and ugly and has large breasts, which combination gets her bullied.

She is a Biker and becomes very good at it, earning the title the 'Best Trouble-shooter In The Business.' Although she is small, she is tough and also pragmatic and naturally very strong, both physically and mentally; her Party trick is picking up a Power Unit with one hand.

Some of Janie's life is planned in meticulous detail, like both her jobs; and some just happens, like her first, unexpected, but torrid love affaire and a tiny act of kindness towards a friend that switches on a complete career change.

For the rich and beautiful, who's main fear is 'Will the media find out?' Janie will be a mystery.

For the other ninety nine percent of us, Janie is what we'd like the girl in our mirror to become:

Local girl made good.

Karen, The Girl That Would Be A Plumber.

She sat at her computer, finishing her report,
-- 'I was just about to test it. My warning was ignored. From that height, a cage in free fall hits the ground at crushing speed.'
She paused, phrasing her next sentence, it would be the final sentence of the account proper, then she just needed to write the Conclusion.
The report was just a few short pages, but, bearing in mind the quality of the hovering silks waiting to present it at the inquest, in effect a 'Get away with Murder' card,
Well -- Manslaughter anyway, she thought.

So begins 'Karen', and we have not yet reached Chapter One. Who has been killed, by whom, how and why is the setting to this unusual erotic novel.

Karen is the most knowledgeable plumber around, except that she isn't a plumber. How and why this oxymoron comes about is the second background theme in this account of the life and loves, testing and success of this feisty Zulu Princess by controversial author, Petra Ceason. The crime fiction whodunit theme running throughout the book, may well keep you guessing until the end.

Once again Miss Ceason challenges the hypocrisy of accepted morality, but this time, up front, as well as close and personal in this latest feel good story.

Delia, Chef In A Wheelchair

Due out in the New Year 2015

Delia Summers is disabled, she needs special ankle supports in a built up right shoe, which she refers to as a Clump. She is a brilliant intuitive cook with an incisive brain, but she does not tolerate fools gladly.

Delia is bright, ruthlessly ambitious and in love with a married man. If that wasn't dangerous enough she's not yet sixteen and the object of desire of the wife her amour.

The scene is set for love and tragedy, intrigue and murder and they are all here in generous portions, hopefully garnished with surprises, chuckles and some laughter on the way.

This is another feel good erotic story from Petra Ceason.

Collected Short Stories And Pomes
{And No, It's Not A Typo.}

Available October 2014

Short stories and Geordie poems {pomes}, that started life as Creative Writing Course homeworks.

Rather than enter them for competitions, where the meaning of the winning prose is too obtuse for me to fathom, or the successful poetry has neither rhyme nor lyricism; I chose to put them in a book where folk could enjoy them for what they are.

A book of short stories usually contains between five and fifteen stories. You are reading about one with sixty of the little critters, ranging in size from fifty to over five thousand words, and believe me, the harder of those two to write was the fifty!

I was kept under severe restraint whilst writing these, gagged; manacled; I'm talking SEVERE restraint here!

So Dear True Reader:-

The sex is understated, and off stage, totally unlike my usual work, but if you like Romance, Crime Fiction, the odd ghost, with just a pinch of fantasy; if you prefer your women feisty, red blooded, even when necessary prepared to do the asking, then this book is for you.

Enjoy,

Petra.

www.ingramcontent.com/pod-product-compliance
Ingram Content Group UK Ltd.
Pitfield, Milton Keynes, MK11 3LW, UK
UKHW041431210726
13854UKWH00010B/1852